I Love Love Walla Walla

Sara Van Donge

Photographs

Sara Van Donge

Joe Drazan, Bygone Walla Walla project

Dedicated to my family. I love you.

I Love Love Walla Walla
Sara Van Donge

Photographs
Sara Van Donge
Joe Drazan, Bygone Walla Walla project

Love song for Walla Walla

I grew up in Walla Walla, the most idyllic, perfect, pristine little town in the most beautiful picturesque part of the entire world. Oh wait. That was someone on TV. That wasn't me. I grew up in a normal town with a very large prison (located on 1313 S 13th Street) and a dead downtown, located in a forgotten corner of a forgotten state. I was a lot like other kids, though my parents were divorced in a time when not that many parents were divorced. I wasn't rich like the cool kids. I was neither pretty nor ugly nor particularly good at sports. I was fairly smart, but only at things like reading and art, not things that people cared about like math or science. But I wasn't miserable or uncool, I was just normal. Your plain old regular person.

But I had something special, something I didn't know was amazing and has saved my behind throughout my life. I had a family, a great big huge extended family. Imperfect and not always there and sometimes frustrating but …. A Family. And no, we aren't Italian or Mexican or Irish, even though a lot of really great Italian and Mexican and Irish families are all around us. In fact we're just a mishmash of different nationalities, a little Dutch, a little German, a little English, and, yes, a little Irish. It would be cool if we had some neat ethnicity, being just white might sound boring and bland, but it's not. Like my grandma, who we call Nanny, likes to say, we're "Full-Blooded American".

I always enjoyed visiting my great-grandparents, well, their graves at least. I have always loved the beauty and tranquility of our lovely Walla Walla cemetery; the enormous trees, the somber tombstones, the complete lack of electronics or machines. I remember the first time I came across my great-grandparents on Cypress street in the cemetery: I was 19 and was at a point in my life when I wasn't sure what I wanted. I was just about to graduate with my bachelor's degree and I felt like I had to make too many decisions and didn't know how. Where to live? What kind of job to pursue? Who to be with? This can be a hard time for young people; I have always wondered why we have to make such long-term decisions at such a young age. I had ridden my bike and ended up at the cemetery and found myself just slowly walking, thinking, crying, when I happened to glance down at one of the graves. I hadn't really been reading the epitaphs at this point, but I was suddenly standing over a grave that said my own name on it: Van Donge. I was shocked to discover I had accidentally found my Grandpa Millerd's parents. I sat down and just talked and talked to them, and I ended up feeling so, so much better. It was cathartic. Later, I learned my Grandma Esther's parents are only a few feet away, so now I visit both graves.

I have visited the cemetery every Memorial Day for as long as I can remember. I used to visit with my grandparents and parents, now it is with my dad and kids and sometimes with cousins. We don't put flowers on the graves, instead my dad brings everyone's favorite candy to sprinkle on their graves. My kids love this because they get to eat candy the whole afternoon (actually, we all love this) and for all of us it is fun to talk about our loved ones and their favorite sweets. We have so many relatives – stretching back to Joseph Weaver many generations ago – that we could easily spend the entire day. It is always interesting to visit my own grave plot, too! Many of my relatives and I bought grave sites when my mom's dad, Fafa, died a few years ago so we could all be buried in the same area. I like knowing that I own a little real estate, the ultimate security.

We have some other family history related to the Mountain View Cemetery because my dad dug graves there before I was born. One of our favorite campfire stories is when my dad was digging a grave at dusk and he had to get inside the grave to make sure the edges were all even so the casket could enter easily. Depending on the fear level of the audience he has two alternate endings.

One: he noticed it was getting darker and the cemetery around him had grown eerily silent. He heard a slight noise above him and looked up to see a crow, just sitting at the edge, looking down at him. Just at that second he heard a loud thump behind him. He turned to find the casket from the plot next to this had settled and fallen a bit into the grave he was digging.....eeeeeeek!

Two: starts about the same, but in this one my dad had gotten in and couldn't get out. A second man falls in after him and when my dad asked how he planned to get out the man suddenly became capable of jumping the five feet to escape. ....ha! This second story may or may not be true.

My uncles, Dean and Barry, also had an adventure in the cemetery. They were commissioned to cut down two trees in the Odd Fellows section, with the resulting fire wood as payment, but they had to do it carefully and not damage any headstones. The plan was for Dean to climb the tree, loop a rope over the limb like a pulley, then tie the rope around a short section of limb. Then when he cut the limb with the chain saw, it could be lowered to the ground. Barry meanwhile would remain on the ground holding the other end of the rope so he could lower the limb safely down among the headstones. But Barry decided to tie the rope around his waist, to add just the right tension to the limb. About that time their dad Millerd, and Uncle Bardell came by to see how the wood cutting was going. Dean cut through the short but deceptively heavy limb which weighed more than Barry did. The result was that the limb just barely slowed down as it fell while Barry, secure to the rope, suddenly bounded across the cemetery, nimbly leaping over headstones at the same rate as the limb's acceleration,. Millerd and Bardell were too overcome with laughter to offer any help. But it was OK, somehow no headstone had been damaged.

I'm thankful for the beauty of our local cemetery. I love to take my kids there to visit or just to ride bikes. As my children grow up I hope I am teaching them the value of knowing where they come from, honoring the past, and showing respect for their ancestors. And maybe that the cemetery doesn't have to be all grief and sadness. Candy and silly stories can also be a part of life and death.

Ice Cream

Like all people, my life has had it's ups and downs. I've suffered the horrible indignity of not making the high school cheer squad (what? Isn't that a major life trauma?). I've been married and abandoned with two small babies (yes, this was a genuine life trauma). And my family may not have been ideal, they may have passed out the jello shots at times instead of the kleenex or they may have just quietly attended the soccer game and not really talked about the ex-husband. But the important thing is that my great big family is all here, in this smallish town and they care. They love me. They might not always say they love me or hug me, they might not show up at everything. But over the years, I can rely on them.

My dad, Greg, was born here in 1950. He's the third boy in a family of four boys and a youngest sister. A family of farmers, the Van Donge family lived on a large farm to the South of town. Their dad and his younger brother worked hard to raise their sons to NOT have to be farmers. When the kids grew up Millerd and Bardel sold the farm and gave what they believed to be a better life to their sons: town life. We all still sigh about it. Oh well. But my dad gave me the best gift a little girl could ever receive: the gift of a loving, kind, dependable dad. He retired after a long successful career as a fireman and is not only cool and fun but also really loving and funny. I am lucky, I hit the lottery with my dad.

My Grandpa Millerd Van Donge, Gramps to all his grandchildren, moved to Walla Walla as a senior in high school from Cove, Oregon during the depression in 1929. His father Bardell had moved the family; his wife Ethel and their four children, to escape a mortgage on a section of farmland, trading the section for 30 acres of strawberries south of Walla Walla free and clear. Millerd was the second oldest son and, after graduating from WaHi, worked on the farm and also for the Union Bulletin Newspaper as a pressman. He met a proof reader at the Union Bulletin named Esther Cole and they were married in 1940. Their third son of five children is my dad who talks fondly of memories of growing up in Walla Walla in the 1950's at places that no longer exist except in memory and old photos. One story that I remember hearing from my dad was about a place called Roedel's Ice Cream Parlor. On Sundays my dad's family went to church at the White Temple Baptist Church, another place that's no longer there. The children would be given 10 or 15 cents for an offering which they would sometimes 'conveniently' forget to drop into the coffers. By prior collaboration my dad and one or two of his brothers would play hooky from church and go to Roedel's. Their favorite concoction was a Cherry Phosphate with a scoop of ice cream in it. They would drink their Phosphate slowly and beg the soda jerk to refill their half full glasses with more soda water to stretch their dimes worth of illicit treat.

Today Walla Walla still has excellent ice cream offerings. Yes, we have a DQ, but one of the best things about Walla Walla is the success of our local shops and restaurants. I think this is one of the main reasons our little town in the middle of nowhere wins Best Small Town contests and has so many successful wine tasting venues. For my family, getting ice cream now is a toss up between Brights and the Patisserie. Brights, located right on Main Street downtown, is cheerful and nostalgic, a charming blend of upscale gifts and homemade candy. At Brights my children, Natalie and Noah, press their noses to the glass as I read them the flavors. I generally encourage them to get one of my favorites - any variation of chocolate - so I can have a bite (hey, if I don't have my own, it doesn't count, right?). I worked here just before going to college and, to this day, I will not eat divinity. I managed to only overdo this one candy, though, so I'm winning.

The Colville Street Patisserie is also downtown and is a different type of environment, more elegant and subdued. Instead of candy and ice cream they specialize in pastries and gelato. Here Natalie and Noah get to taste little samples, though they rarely branch out from chocolate or vanilla. I may even get my own cup here since small portions are available. Gelato is different from ice cream - smoother somehow and not as sweet. I was lucky enough to have gelato in Italy and the Patisserie's is equally delicious.

Ice cream continues as a family tradition today. In the summertime my dad and my cousin Drew both make ice cream. We all agree the hand-cranked machine is a better choice, mainly because the electric ice cream machine is so loud. A couple of years ago Drew brought his electric ice cream maker to my house for a party. He sealed it up in the kitchen while we all enjoyed our food out on the back porch. The thing was so loud that no one would even enter the kitchen. In fact my cousin Abbie didn't know what it was and was too nervous to even enter my house at all! Today the hand-cranked machines can be harder to find, but getting together with family and friends and taking turns cranking the ice cream is fun. In fact, any excuse to eat ice cream is fun.

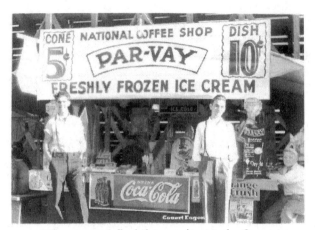

Where can I find these prices today?

Whitman

Remnants of my tongue may still remain on the giant paperclip on the Whitman College Campus. I have lived on or near Whitman College the majority of my life. As a young child my mom was the head resident at

North Hall and later at Jewett Hall. My older brother and I had a glorious childhood living on the campus surrounded by the college kids. But being an older brother, Christian couldn't let me grow up unscathed, which was probably why he encouraged me to stick my tongue to the frozen paperclip sculpture. Of course, like Ralphie in the Christmas Movie, my tongue froze to the metal. My mom likes to tell the story of my brother and our good friend Jay Van Dyke running into the dining hall right at dinner to inform my mom of my mishap. Of course all the college students had to run out and see, since I was like everyone's little sister. By the time they got outside I was running in, blood dripping all over my winter coat. The only consolation was getting to see that little piece of my tongue stuck to the sculpture for weeks after.

Despite this one lapse of judgment, I loved living there; we had so many exciting things going on at all times. People throwing coins from windows! Food fights in the cafeteria! Sorority girls dressed like Pink Ladies! I was lucky enough to live at Whitman until I was 6 and I really enjoyed it. My mom always had cookies in her antique apple-shaped cookie jars, so the college students would often stop by for a visit. Whitman College is such a benefit to our little town. When I lived there the students were adults to me, but as time has passed and I get older they stay the same age.

Our first residence hall was North Hall, previously General Hospital where I was born. To say North Hall is creepy is an understatement. We had to enter in the dark basement and work our way upstairs past endless doors and flickering fluorescent lights, past old operating rooms and dark stairwells. It seems appropriate that, years later, North Hall was the site of a successful Haunted Hospital at Halloween. It was put on by Whitman students and included a doctor with a chain saw, scary people in masks, and lots of creepy sounds. But as a place to live North Hall was wonderful – we had the top floor, full of windows and huge ceilings. I had an x-ray screen in my room, there was a ramp for our big wheels, and we even had a roof – which my mom says I jumped off, good thing I don't remember that!

Soon after my 7th birthday we moved to a house near Whitman College, so I still felt like I was part of the campus. My best friend, Erin Johnson, and I spent many happy afternoons hiding in trees and bushes all over Whitman, pretending to be abandoned orphans. My friends and I also fed the ducks, played Capture the Flag, and went on scavenger hunts around the college. It was our own park, the students, weddings, and academic pursuits were just background noise to us.

I remember as a college student I would come home and - amazing! - these college students were suddenly my age. I snuck into a couple of large parties at the Tau Kappa Epsilon (TKE) house and other Fraternities during weekend visits home. As a life-long townie, my main focus at these parties was admiring the houses, since I had rarely been inside any building on the campus. To this day I pay attention to these beautiful houses on campus. In fact I noticed the big TKE house was recently repainted.

Now the college kids are....kids. I still live very close to campus and they walk by my house at all hours. I see them now as studious, creative, responsible kids, completely different from how I saw them a few decades ago. No longer do I chase them around and try to meet them. Or holler at them from bushes. Or try to get invited to their parties. No, now they are just students, young people beginning their lives.

But Whitman campus remains relatively the same. Sure, it continuously evolves and changes, the grounds and buildings are kept up and improved at an impressive rate. But it is still my own private park, my jogging path, a playground for my own children. Thanks for being there Whitman, you make Walla Walla even more beautiful.

Shack Sweet Shack

I didn't just live with my mom, I also lived with my dad. Though I feel like I had a relatively stable and happy childhood, we moved around a lot after my parents got divorced. By the time I graduated from high school I had moved nine times, though once it was away from and then back into the same house. I never minded too much, we were all together and in Walla Walla, so I was happy. One of the most memorable places, though, was when my dad lived in the shack.

It really was a shack. A one-room, uninsulated little house located about a mile from my grandparents house. The shack was where migrant workers lived when they helped Gramps and Bardel with harvest. My mom can still get a little worked up when she remembers how my dad moved there after their divorce, especially because at one point I stepped on a nail. Barefoot. But stuff like this doesn't matter, a mere nail in the foot on the way to the outhouse is nothing. Pshaw! Moms can be so uptight. My brother Christian and I were happy visiting my dad at the shack. The irony of the shack was that he had an enormous, expensive waterbed we all shared and it was so comfortable and cozy. I have fond memories of those brief days.

My favorite, though, was when we lived with my grandparents. Nanny and Fafa were wonderful, the kind of grandparents I hope to be someday. Indulgent and kind, stable and attentive, I loved that year my mom was going to school. But then she became a nurse and bought a house, so we moved again. But my Nanny made dinner every single Sunday at noon, my entire childhood. Through all the moves and unpredictability, Nanny and Fafa's house always felt like home to me.

In fact I hit the lottery with both my parents. It took me longer to appreciate my mom, as it does with most mothers and daughters I imagine. My mom, Linda, also grew up in Walla Walla. She was the oldest of four, two younger sisters and a younger brother. Her family is not docile, religious, and quiet like my dad's. Her parents drank and smoked and danced and sang and had a ton of fun. But being the oldest daughter in a family of fun-loving parents made her naturally very hard working and task oriented. As a kid, I resented my mom always being the one to make me bathe, turn in homework, write thank you cards. Ugh, the same stuff I do for my kids today. But, like I said, I got pretty lucky getting a mom like this. What better way to grow up than with a fun dad and a hard-working mom?

Unless, of course, they get divorced and remarry and neither step-parent is a home-run. Darn, that gave me a little trauma. But not too much, I wasn't abused or anything. Just slightly hurt because I had two different homes and the sadness of missing my intact family and the worse sadness of seeing my parents even more miserable the second time. No small things, pain those of us who endure it carry around as lumps in our hearts and throats. Maybe this is why, when I got married too young to the wrong man I stayed married even though it was clearly a huge error. I figured if my parents should have stayed married then I should too.

Kid Food

I have always loved school lunches, even today I get to eat school lunches once or twice a week, though I usually try to bring leftovers from home. When I was a little girl my Nanny was a school cook, and for one year we were at the same elementary school. I was so proud of this! I loved seeing her there in the kitchen when I would go in and get my lunch, plus she would always sneak me a little something extra. The best day was chili which included a maple bar. She would often find an extra maple bar for me, earning me the admiration of my classmates.

In the fifth grade we got to work in the cafeteria, a job I loved. We got to leave class (math, yes!) a few minutes early and go down to the cafeteria and do jobs like take milk money or lunch tickets, collect dirty trays, or my favorite, wash pots and pans. Why this was my favorite is beyond me, but I think it was because I was actually doing a real job. We started with great big dirty pots then washed them until they were genuinely clean. All this for the payment of a free lunch? This was my kind of job! My family didn't even need the free lunch, I just liked earning something for myself.

I loved most school lunches and they catered to little kid tastes: fish sticks, hamburgers and tater tots, canned fruits with little dollops of whipped cream. Even at home my Nanny was really nice about preparing kid-friendly food. Unlike my parents who always prepared boringly healthy sit-down meals consisting of meat, a fresh vegetable, and a whole-grain starch with milk to drink, my Nanny and Fafa's house was loaded with processed junk food. Coca-cola, Hostess treats (my favorite was the ChocoBliss, mmmmm), Wonder Bread, Steak-ums ("Move over bacon, now there's something meatier!"), and Miracle Whip. If it was unhealthy and delicious we got to eat it. Sugary cereals, a whole cupboard! Cocoa Puffs! Frooty Pebbles! Cap'n Crunch! Plus my Fafa loved to make us Chocolate Milkshakes when we watched movies at night. It's a wonder we didn't get sick.

Compared to the extreme health food at home and the extreme indulgence at my grandparents, school lunches were juuust right. A little processed meat, a little canned vegetable, some milk, a small amount of something sweet. All served on an individual tray - mine was always, always blue. Always. In six years of hot lunches I managed to always snag a coveted blue tray, no orange or brown for me. It was a class project sometimes, since my classmates knew my record they would even pass the scarce blue tray to me if there weren't many in the pile. I had nice classmates.

In elementary school we got to be Patrols or Crossing Guards too, a fun job reserved for sixth graders. This was a great privilege, something every kid wanted to do. Getting to put on the bright orange vest and holding up the patrol flag made us so official and mature; the little kids all admired us. This was a job that held more clout than Cafeteria worker, even though for me wasn't really as fun. But, being me and being young and wanting to fit in, I stuck with patrol.

Sara Van Donge

Fafa's Chocolate Milkshake

Fafa's Famous Milkshake

Ingredients:
Whole Milk
Vanilla Ice Cream
Chocolate Sauce

Fill a glass nearly full with vanilla ice cream. Add a large squirt of chocolate sauce. Pour in milk until it is barely visible at the top of the ice cream. Stir until it is a nice thick consistency, adding more milk if necessary. Share with all the little kids you care about.

Variation:
Coke milkshake: Substitute Coca-Cola for milk, either with or without chocolate sauce.

Mean kids

It wasn't always easy to fit in, though when I was younger I didn't notice the times I didn't. Until I was in the 6th grade I hadn't realized there was such a thing as cool and uncool and that a person's clothes had anything to do with this. I imagined I was hip and savvy and my clothes allowed me to fit in.

I was wearing a new outfit, one I had saved my babysitting money to buy: acid washed jeans and a matching jean jacket plus new turquoise tennis shoes like everyone seemed to be wearing that fall. I was really proud of those shoes, I had just purchased them the weekend before at Kmart. They didn't look exactly like everyone else's, it seemed a lot of kids had some black writing inside the little white circle on the ankle, but my plain white circle was just as cute and the shoes were my favorite color, so what did it matter? It mattered. Our boys team was playing a basketball game that afternoon against the school across town, and I was staying after school with all my friends to watch the game. I had run out to the front of the building to check in with my mom and was just running back inside, I felt pretty cute as I ran up the front steps toward the gym. I noticed two boys from the other school lounging against the railing of the steps watching me approach.

"Nice Fake Converse," one sneered as I ran past.

I wanted to stop, my heart lurched for a moment, but I kept going. Fake Converse? Was that what my shoes were supposed to be called? I entered the crowded gym and found a spot next to Erin.

"Are my shoes Converse?" I asked her.

She didn't even have to look at them, she just knew, "No, they just look like Converse. Why?" Erin was watching her boyfriend Jeff Eng as he dribbled the ball around during warm-ups. She wasn't at all concerned about my shoes being fake.

I was mortified, like I had done something wrong. I told her about the cruel tone of the boy outside. She shook her head, "That's Prospect Point for you," she said, "snobs."

Even though my friend didn't seem bothered by the lameness of my shoes, I was embarrassed. That boy, with his three unkind words, had turned my feeling of belonging and confidence into insecurity. Suddenly I doubted myself, my ability to fit in. What else was I wearing that inspired others' scorn?

Thankfully most of the students at Green Park were either not wealthy or, like Erin, had parents who were too sensible to allow them to be materialistic. My elementary classmates had little use for the shallow values this sorry young boy displayed. But I wasn't off the hook. When we entered Junior High in 7th grade things changed drastically. I'm not sure if this was because of the students we were now going to school with or simply what happens to people when they get to be about thirteen years old, but suddenly what we wore mattered. A lot. People I went to school with felt it was their right to make snide comments about other people's clothing, often related to it's price. For girls it was Guess jeans. Somehow having that tiny little triangle on the back pocket of the jeans was a big priority, and if it was fake, like Jordache, other people could and would laugh and make fun of you. The pressure was painful, especially for those of us who didn't have parents who paid for whatever clothing we wanted on a whim.

By the time I was in high school I stopped even trying, I discovered the joy of shopping at Goodwill and expressing myself artistically with my clothing. Not to mention saving my babysitting money for things that mattered, like skiing, going to a movie.....college.

My kids and I still love Converse

Rope Swing

Our Pearson Street house (the one we moved out of and then back to) had a rope swing. I'm not talking about a skinny little 10 foot rope, prickly and hard to sit on, like the sad and neglected ropes I see dangling from small trees around town. Also not like the too-thick, heavily-supervised ropes we used to have in school gyms. No, this rope swing was ideal in every way. From the smooth feel of the white rope to the perfect size of the knot for sitting or standing, our rope swing was perfect. My dad and older brother hung the rope from the high sturdy branch of one of our Sycamore trees in the parking strip. I estimate it was at least 20 feet long; it was easily higher than the roof of our two story house, so it had a long smooth trajectory from our porch out over the patio almost over the street. Because of its length, the ride was slow and lasted for usually three big swings – the initial exciting jump, followed by a slightly shorter return, and ending by one slower swing back toward the middle of the patio.

On special occasions – days when we had no school or obligations and when the weather was beautiful – my dad would bring out the ladder. The excitement! He would lean the ladder against the house, allowing us to climb up the second story, step out onto the eave of the porch roof and leap onto the rope. Now this was a big swing! A huge swoop with the rope beginning in the form of a J but straightening smoothly into an arc across the patio toward the opposite end of the patio. No matter how many times I did it, I never lost the thrilling feeling of having my stomach drop out from under me. Oh! How I would love to do that again. The house is no longer in our family; my dad sold it right after I graduated from high school. I brought a friend by it recently. As I was describing the rope and the Sycamores, I stepped backwards towards one, expecting to feel the tree. Instead I stepped into nothing. The trees were gone, replaced by baby trees that may someday grow big enough to have enormous rope swings of their own.

When I was in college, I wrote this poem about the rope swing:

Rush

Long distant ladder
my right hand destination
rope clenched in my left
a flying leap
landing
hanging
between rope and ladder
suspended

Feet
forward
one-handed ascent
Toward the roof
shaking
wobbling
turning
around
slowly
(don't drop the heavy rope hard ground so far below)

clutching
jumping
sailing
across the patio

over the sidewalk
within inches of the somber Sycamore tree
     arcing back suspended mid-air

A disturbing story about my poem. I submitted it to our school magazine and they published it. My first published writing! A few weeks later I ran into one of the editors at a party. He was really impressed with my poem, he said they were intrigued by it because it was about .... suicide. I did not let on how disturbed I was that he misread my poem so completely. I don't want to think about suicide, it is too intense to even contemplate and I am thankful and lucky I don't really have the right to be discussing it. That this editor thought my poem was this deep bothered me, maybe so much that I've never really shared any poetry since. Who knows what they might think it means.

Or maybe poetry is supposed to be deep? Some of my poems are pretty dark and sad, in fact now that my life is relatively calm and turmoil free I don't even write poetry any more at all. There was a time about ten years ago when I was unhappily married and wouldn't admit it even to myself when poems seemed to float around my head all the time. I would soothe myself by writing them down, in tight little cursive so no one would see. The editor who liked my one and only published poem would probably like them. Maybe I'll toss a few in here after awhile. Or probably not, ugh. I don't want to be there anymore.

Oh well. I guess not all poetry is really that deep, sometimes it is just what it seems. Sometimes a poem is just a description of a rope swing and a fun afternoon. Although, considering how we no longer have rope swings in any of our school gyms because they are dangerous, it does make jumping off a roof with a rope in your hand seem a little self-harmful. I'm glad I lived to tell the tale.

Green Park

And speaking of poems, here is one a group of fifth and sixth grade students wrote together with our music teacher Phyllis Bonds back in the early 1980's. I could sing it for you if you wanted, in fact if you found anyone from my Green Park class I imagine they could too.

Oh Green Park School is number one
And we have lots and lots of fun
People here are really cool
None of us would be a fool

Patrol, cafeteria, work to be done
Assemblies with awards that we have won
Spelling bees, wrestling are but a few
All-City Basketball Championships too

Oh Green Park School is number one
And we have lots and lots of fun
People here are really great
That's why
(Clap Clap)
We should cel -e- brate!

24

Green Park!

Yes, I attended Green Park Elementary School during the 1980's. Initially we were the Green Park Super Stars, but when Buddy Heimbigner retired, our new principal, Charlene Bailey, invited us to choose a new mascot. My third grade suggestion was the Green Park Gorillas, but Green Park Panthers won out. Oh how I loved Green Park! This was back when the 1952, "Small Building" was still there, before the amazingly well done 1995 remodel. The younger kids, gym/cafeteria/stage, and office were all in the Small Building and only the 5th and 6th graders got to be in the Big Building. It was such an honor to move up to the Big Building! Being in an entirely different building made us feel older than the rest of the students. And the building itself was remarkable – the enormous windows and ceilings, still impressively displayed today; the grand stair case; the creepy basement and boiler room; the forbidden top floor. The forbidden top floor? How enticing is that for 12 year old kids? Of course we would sneak up there to look at the abandoned classrooms, still furnished but dark and dusty.

Today Green Park is a cohesive building – one large structure, no small little portables and prohibited classrooms. I am so grateful for the elegant way they remodeled it, Green Park is still beautiful and spacious though now it is much more comfortable and modern. One thing that remains the same, however, is the Green Park Carnival. Even though my own children do not attend Green Park, I have always brought them to the Green Park Carnival. It is more than just nostalgia; it really is a great carnival. Held in outdoors in May, it is one of our families' long time favorite events. When I was a little girl we had ticket sale contests and one of my proudest moments in life was being a top ticket salesperson. Of course it never occurred to me until adulthood that my enormous family buying all the tickets gave me an unfair advantage….I was just happy to be the best at something!

In the words of our long ago spirit song Green Park School is really great, that's why….we should celebrate! When we had our 10th class reunion I ended up being one of the organizers. I had fun working with my friend Jena renting the Elks, decorating, deciding on food and music. I had less fun tracking down classmates, getting berated by these same classmates by how over-priced it was, and listening to people try to get in for free. But the best part of the whole reunion was the first evening when I decided to invite all my classmates that had gone to Green Park for a barbecue at my house before the informal party at a local bar, The Green. It was so fun to catch up with these kids, these people I had genuinely known as a small child. Some of our favorite teachers even joined us briefly. It was great, and quite frankly it gave us a lot more confidence to walk into that reunion a couple hours later.

The tenth reunion had it's crazy moments. I happened to be five months pregnant so I didn't get to join in the late night antics. But I bore witness, especially when a couple people called me at one in the morning and begged me to drive them home. My lips are sealed on this one though!

Playgrounds

Green Park had a great playgrounds, too. Even today I love playgrounds because my children are so pleased to go to one...while I read a book and chat with other moms. Playgrounds allow all of us to have a good time. And I'll admit, I still really like playing on them. Our favorite game is Zombie Tag, perfect for the swinging bridges, monkey bars, and slides on big playgrounds. Of course I get to be the Zombie and the best part of the game is that I walk around in slow motion so it requires no serious effort. Just an occasional arm swipe and a "rah!" and my kids are deliciously frightened. That's my kind of game.

Remember the extremely dangerous equipment from decades ago that we somehow managed to survive? The merry-go-rounds, teeter-totters, and rope swings that kids of today would never be able to handle without an extra insurance policy? Our largest local park, Pioneer Park, was full of these minefields. I remember (vaguely) a red, four-way bouncy thing where, if you weren't careful, your fingers could get caught in coils of metal. Ouch! And the merry-go-round, where if you sat on the edge, clinging to the bar, you could let go and fly! Or if you were brave you could stand in the middle and not really get dizzy at all. Wildwood Park, on Division, had a teeter-totter. You had to be really careful who you went on with, because if it was a mean, heavy kid you could get trapped at the top. And then dropped. Brutal. We learned a lot about physics on teeter-totters, like if you were with a friend who was slightly lighter you could move forward toward the fulcrum point until you balanced.

Where does all this old equipment go? My cousin, Karie, wondered if maybe it is like the Old Sign Graveyard in Las Vegas. She had a rope swing in her backyard that had previously been at Jefferson School. Remember that place? I can't even get started on the delirium that caused people to tear down that fabulous building. To replace it with a movie theater. Then a video store. Then a parking lot. Sigh.

And of course, everyone's favorite was the big metal twisty slide that was at Prospect Point Elementary School. Before it became a playground mecca it was used as a fire escape. It had no ladder, we had to climb up the slide part in order to slide down. We had to be good communicators, too, because if someone happened to be coming down at the same time someone else was coming up serious injuries could follow. This slide was so big and fun that we would ride our bikes clear across town just to play on it.

Do you see the slide outside Prospect Point? What a fire escape!!

I remember Green Park's playground had two towers connected by a bridge, really fun for little kids. Even more fun for big kids avoiding adult eyes! As 5th and 6th graders we could go up there and have club meetings and private conversations. It gave us a place where we could be free without adult supervision; and of course, this was when kids started to "go out" which was our idea of asking someone to be a girlfriend or boyfriend. Kids would go in the towers in big groups, stand around the designated couple and count to three, then…they would kiss. In front of everyone. Though I never had the nerve to actually do this.

I was cool enough to have a boyfriend around this time, too. His name was Brian and he was the most popular guy in the class. Cute with blonde hair and blue eyes, Brian was good at sports and had an awesome flat-top haircut. Every girl had a crush on him and Brian obligingly went through the rounds of the girls, asking us out and breaking up with us and giving everyone a lot to talk about.

I remember the day Brian first asked me out: Theresa, who seemed to always be enmeshed in everything that was going on but who never actually seemed to have anything going on herself, whispered to me in class that Brian was going to ask me out. I was thrilled! Me??? I glanced across the room at Brian who was uncharacteristically interested in Mrs. Edwards instruction, and throughout the day I kept wondering when this exciting event would take place.

Sure enough, just before afternoon recess, a note suddenly landed on my desk. It was from Brian.

<u>Will you be my girlfriend. Check the box. Yes. No.</u>

Eeeeeek! I was thrilled! There were two boxes drawn on the paper, next to the No was a small box, next to the Yes a great big box. Guess which one I checked?

Brian didn't even wait for me to return the note. He whispered my name and held up his arms, questioning. Well? I nodded, so excited!

We never really spoke, but I was suddenly extra popular for being his girlfriend. The excitement lasted two weeks, during which time the other kids tried to get us to kiss in the tower but neither of us could bring ourselves to do it. Then I received another note, this one was hand-delivered by a smug Theresa, again somehow ingrained in my business.

I want to break up.

"No!" I said, "What if I don't want to?"

Theresa, who had something like five older sisters and knew all about boyfriends, chuckled.

"You have to. If he doesn't want to go out anymore then you can't go out anymore."

I was devastated. I went home and cried for a few minutes until my friend Afton called me, she had heard the news (probably from Theresa). Afton had also been dumped that day, by her boyfriend John. We commiserated for a minute but then cooked up a scheme: we would invent boyfriends! We spent the evening creating boyfriends for ourselves from Assumption, the nearby private school, we gave them names and personalities and even wrote notes to ourselves from them and topped off the falsification by writing their names with hearts around them on our binders.

The next day we put our plan to action, we walked into school with our heads held high, super excited about our new Assumption "boyfriends". We shared our notes from them with anyone who would listen. We completely ignored John and Brian.

And our scheme was a success! Well, if you can call tricking someone into being your boyfriend a success, but we were 11. Both Brian and John sent us new notes asking us out, we both said yes, though this time there was less excitement and it only lasted a few days. But no matter, I had experienced my first love affair.

Cupid's Arrow

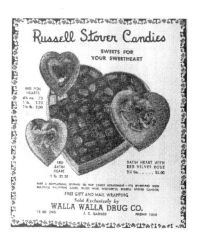

I used to be someone's Secret Admirer. I cringe when I think about how this must have felt for the poor fifth grade boy who was the unwilling recipient of my love letters, but cupid's arrow hit me hard and I was a slave to my love.

I'm too embarrassed even all these years later to even say his name, though if any one of my girlfriends are reading this she will shake her head and laugh and know exactly who it is. That's how lame I was about this boy, so foolishly in love that I talked on and on about him to anyone who would listen, for years. I remember the moment I first decided this boy was the boy for me. I was in the 6th grade and loving life, Erin Johnson and I were totally cool and tearing it up as the oldest kids in the school. We had just walked out of the school one fall afternoon and were headed to the bike rack for our bikes, and there he was.

I had never seen him before and for whatever reason I decided he was the cutest boy I had ever seen. I was instantly love struck. From that moment on my first priority was a mixture of stalking this poor guy while simultaneously living in fear that I might someday actually have to speak to him. I was in trouble and I seriously doubt he had any idea, at least I hope he didn't!

But somehow after a couple of weeks of just watching him play football across the playground or looking for him in the cafeteria, I decided it was time to take action and write him a love letter. I slaved over this letter and the half-dozen subsequent letters I inflicted on the innocent kid. I don't remember what I wrote, but I do know it was pretty long and, like the conscientious writer I was born to be, I first wrote a rough draft then revised and made changes and edited and didn't rewrite it onto pretty stationery until I was certain it conveyed the perfect sentiment. I do remember using my favorite notecards (horror of horror!) they were light blue, two little bears playing together under a tree and that I used my favorite blue pen and my best handwriting. Then in a stroke of brilliance I signed it 'Your Secret Admirer.'

The next morning I made sure to get to school extra early so I could hide the love letter in his desk. I snuck into his classroom and looked around for the desk with his name tag on it, where I carefully placed the envelope addressed to him. Then I dashed to my own classroom down the hall, waiting in anticipation for...what? I'm not sure, I certainly wouldn't have been able to deal with it if he had actually liked me back.

This is how I entertained myself for a lot of sixth grade, and thankfully nothing actually came of it. However, at Halloween I had the tiniest glimmer of recognition from him. What happened was that I decided we should have a Halloween party and that it should be for all the fifth and sixth grade students. Of course I had an obvious ulterior motive, I wanted this cupid's arrow guy to show up and maybe, I don't know, ask me to dance or something? I don't know, I never really got that far. But as we were putting together the Halloween party I kept insisting the fifth graders also be included, an idea none of the other girls planning could understand. Finally someone asked point blank if I liked a boy in the fifth grade. What could I do but admit it? Besides, up until this point I hadn't been able to tell anyone except Erin and I longed to declare my new love to the world.

Theresa got involved again. Remember Theresa? The same girl who meddled in my "relationship" with Brian the year before? Well now she had new fodder for her life of living vicariously through other people and she wasn't going to just let this one be. My friends, goaded by Theresa, got the idea that they should make the party for all sixth graders plus this one boy. Just him. I was appalled! Since I was the main instigator of the party I was certain he would know all about my secret crush and my whole life of mystery stalker, love-letter writer would come to an end.

My objections were totally ignored, in fact they physically forced me out onto the playground while they made and put up a poster for the event. Then with great smiles of triumph they presented the poster to me:

Halloween Party!
All Sixth Graders and (the boy's name) Invited
This Saturday Night
The Green Park Gym

As I stood in the hallway reading this poster, feeling both indignation mixed with a thrill that we had actually done something bold for this boy, I realized this very boy was standing right next to me. And he was smiling!

So I did what any totally inept sixth grader would do, I reached up and tore the poster off the wall and ran away. And when later he didn't show up to the party (really? Like he would after that invitation?) I was relieved more than anything.

And I think I managed to avoid speaking to the cupid's arrow boy for at least three years. Oh, I sent him the occasional love letter still. And on Valentine's Day I even had Erin deliver one to him in person and he told her to tell me I was cute. But I still never talked to him, it was just more comfortable that way.

Schools have changed

School has changed from when we were kids. A lot. The way teachers treat students has changed, especially from the time my parents were in school (paddle, anyone?) The way students treat each other is also quite different. And our state and federal interventions cause a lot of changes. The demands placed on kids (and subsequently schools) now are astronomical in comparison to what we dealt with in school or even compared to what kids had to think about 16 years ago. But technology may be the number one difference. When I first began teaching in 1997 I had an overhead projector in my room, a great big R2-D2 of a machine that stood in the middle of my room and let me write with colored pens on a piece of plastic so I could show an entire room information instead of having to walk around and show them one by one. It would also project anything that was see-through, so for teaching math I could show shapes or quantities and in reading I could use special paper to copy articles so students could see what I was reading or follow along with main ideas. It was useful and allowed students to see what I was teaching, but it was much more time-intensive than the document camera and projector I have today. I liked it though, it was a compact work station and allowed me to still be in the middle of my classroom teaching while being able to present information to everybody at once.

Way back in 1997 I didn't have a computer or even a telephone in my classroom, and I was OK! If there was something important that needed to be conveyed to me the secretary would announce it over the intercom or send a student office helper up with a note. We took attendance on a piece of paper and sent it down to the office. Any information that needed to be given to us from a parent, the school, the district, or the state was placed in our mailboxes to be dealt with after school. I got, on average, one or two messages in my mailbox a day. How many messages do we get in our mailbox each day now? Ha ha ha, I'm not really laughing. When I taught in those years, I didn't have a desk in my room, I spent the entire day walking around the classroom. When I sat down it was next to a student, to give specialized instruction or to join in a game or a conversation. When I read a book to the class I had to walk around the room while I read it so everyone could see the pictures. Students had me near them most of the time, there was not much opportunity to hide out in the back of the room; there was no back of the room.

I remember when our school district first started purchasing document cameras for people, I was pretty wary about this new technology. Even though I generally embrace new ideas and technology is something I'm comfortable learning to use, this new system was really complex. A spindly-looking camera with about fifteen buttons labeled only with icons was connected by cords to a space-age box. The box has it's own remote control decked out with probably sixty buttons labeled with mysterious words like angle and marker and random and standby and input all connected to my computer screen (oops, not screen, monitor, it's called a monitor) and then again to the actual computer. Cords snake endlessly around my desk, so many cords that they are covered by a ten-inch wide strip of vinyl to prevent anyone from accidentally pulling something out. Me being confused and overwhelmed by this system had nothing to do with my age at the time (I was 26) or education level (I had a Master's degree in Information and Technology). I can safely say that the amount and sophistication of technology in our classrooms is massive. This is not a complaint or a boast, simply an observation.

This new system is now standard; as far as I know our school district has been able to outfit every single classroom in Walla Walla with this set up, allowing all teachers to simply press some buttons and, voila!

their students even in the fifth row can easily see the caption they are referring to in the text book. It is impressive. I am an advanced Spanish teacher, I don't just teach people body parts and days of the week. I teach advanced grammar but through concepts that are interesting so they are learning vocabulary at the same time. We read books about Ancient Greece in order to practice past tense verbs. We study world problems and read articles from CNN Mexico to in order to practice the potential simple tense (if I could … I would…). So our technology allows me to look up concepts on the computer and show them to my students. We are studying the effects of globalization on indigenous people in Costa Rica? We can see a youtube video comparing an environmental landmark before and after a new industry comes in. We are learning about pyramids in Ancient Egypt? We can see photographs of the pyramids taken by satellite. Technology opens up the world.

But I wonder what it does to relationships? Now I have to make a concerted effort to come out from behind the computer. I force myself not to look at emails while class is going on by turning off the notification button. I make sure to turn the projector off and walk among the students whenever they are writing or actively working on a project. Obviously, no cell phones are allowed in class. I've taken training classes and been at meetings where the presenter doesn't explicitly demand this and adults will have their cell phones out on the table. It doesn't take long for some people to be so absorbed by their little screens that they might as well not even be in the class at all.

Yet, I'm as bad as the rest. I know exactly where my phone is at this moment and how many messages I need to respond to and how far behind I am on my email. I sit on my couch at night while my kids watch their cartoon after dinner and I check Facebook. I can't break free anymore than anyone else. It is a brave new world and I wonder if any of us will ever be the same.

But not all school changes are so overwhelming, in fact when my parents describe some of the indignity they went through in school I am grateful for the distraction of too many cords or too many state standards. Back in the 1950's kids didn't seem to have the same influence that they have today, they were silent unless spoken to and adults were always right. My dad has mentioned more than once a teacher who would hit them on the knuckles with a wooden ruler when they were doing anything she didn't like. Man, the only thing I ever used a ruler for in school besides measuring was making fake fingernails by putting glue down that middle strip. No teacher would have ever hit me with one!

My mom told me they used to practice for a potential A-Bomb evacuation. The alarm would go off...and they were to run home. Bye-bye, be safe now. Uh, ok. We don't get to be that flippant with our charges, 1950's, wow. My dad has a similar story. He was a young elementary student and got sick at school. The school wasn't able to get ahold of his mom at home, so they just told him to walk home. He lived on a farm about two miles away. It was early spring and he decided to take a short-cut by crossing a river, he got chest deep and felt himself being lifted and almost carried downstream but managed to swim to safety on the other side. He then had to walk, sick and wet, the rest of the way home. Again, nicely done 1950's, way to care for the Baby Boomers. Good job, no wonder many grew up and became hippies and didn't trust the government.

Then of course there was discipline. When I was going to school in the 1980's teachers were nice, even when kids were kind of difficult. I guess I was in a class with a lot of boys that were not easy to teach; when I became a teacher two of my previous teachers laughed when they remembered how hard my class had been. But I never really noticed, the worst thing that would ever happen was that the teacher might make someone write their name on the board. Or if they were really bad they had to put a check after their name and stay after school, with their head down. Whoa, big time punishment. When I was in elementary school there was a boy in the other class who didn't like this check system, I will call him Harvey. Harvey had a little trouble following directions, and he lost it one day to such an extent that other kids were talking about it for weeks afterward. The teacher told him to put his name on the board, as she did every day. And, like every day Harvey had to put a check after his name too. Harvey frequently had to put even a second check, but this day when the teacher told him to put a second check Harvey stalked up there and put check after check after check, each check getting bigger and bigger. He was like some kind of hero the way he rebelled against the teacher, though as a teacher now my heart aches for him. He must have felt terrible to always have his name on the board.

My parents' generation and even my older brothers' generation had the threat of the paddle looming over their heads, and this actually trickled down to us. We would whisper that someone was going to get the paddle but no one ever did, in fact by the time I was in school it was illegal, but we didn't know this. Now it is a totally forgotten idea. We treat kids with dignity, speaking to them quietly, keeping carefully documented record of any misbehavior and informing parents and counsellors of even the most minor behavior infraction. It works because the kids are informed and are required to take ownership of the whole situation, from telling us what their behavior was and why when we fill out the paperwork to making the phone call themselves to their parents. There is no public shaming or physical punishment. Thank goodness, we've come a long way. But we're not perfect, I wonder what they'll find to complain about when they look back on us 20 years from now?

Science Instruction at Green Park in 1957

Hair and style

My mom, Linda, and her friend Rhonda. Note the 70's hair.

In 1988 big hair was in, in fact if you were in junior high in 1988 big hair was essential. My hair, being naturally straight, chose not to follow the trend, no matter how I tried. All the really stylish girls had this big, sticky, curly hair like a foamy cloud around their faces. I longed to have my hair look like this, enduring perms that fell out after one wash, sponge curlers, hair spray, and crimping irons. I never liked ratting my hair, but I realize now this was the one element missing from my styling regimen. In the 7th grade I played on the JV basketball team (I use the word play loosely here, more accurately I cheered from the bench). Our practices were held before school, giving us the opportunity to get ready together as a team in the morning. One morning, my friends Alison and Stephanie asked if they could attempt to make my hair look curly and cool. I hesitated before allowing them to try – by this point I had given up on ever having big hair and had resigned myself to just enjoying big sticky bangs. But I finally relented, mainly out of curiosity. These two had so much fun with my hair! As I walked down the hall with big Madonna hair I felt so chic…but when it came to recreating the time-consuming style I just didn't have it in me, so the next day I was back to my straight, uncool hair.

Now if I had been born twenty years earlier I would have had hair to be envious of. My mom and my godmother, Connie, both had stick-straight hair parted down the middle. In the 1960's this was the grooviest hair imaginable. I would have fit right in. Plus, who doesn't love bell-bottoms and leather-fringed vests? Compared to the billowy neon we wore in the 1980's the styles of my mom's generation are sleek and flattering.

Rockin' the 1970's styles: My dad, top right, with his brother Dean. Bottom left, his brother Barry, their cousin Connie, and brother Jerry.

But the early 1990's – now there was a style I could do. Grunge. Remember grunge? Not just the music, which we trained ourselves to love despite its furious and non-melodious rant, but the style. No makeup. Hair in whatever ratty bun or braid or whatever it felt like doing. Dirty flannels over baggy jeans. Or if we were dressing up and not being all hip and grungy then we might get fancy with colored jeans and matching jean jacket. Bright blue or magenta. I'm not really sure what happened to young people at that time, but this may have been a direct response to the over-done look of the previous generation.

Sports Star

Where I went to school being athletic was very important if you wanted to fit in and be popular. Forget about having any social clout if you lumbered around like a big klutz. So I made every effort to be a sports star.

Now I wasn't terrible by any means, but I wasn't exactly what you would call good. I am now, as an adult, more of an individual type of athlete: good at biking, hiking, dancing at parties, yoga. But I got it in my head somehow about the age of twelve that in order to be truly cool and popular I needed to be an amazing all-start athlete. This may have stemmed directly from reading too many Sweet Valley High books and watching Can't Buy Me Love too many times, but my idea of junior high school success was the jocks wearing the letterman jacket. And I was going to be one of those jocks.

Forget that I was raised by a mom who did not watch or talk about or participate in any sports ever (unless you count aerobics classes) and by a dad who considered biking and camping the only two really important sports in the world. Closely followed by cross-country skiing and rock climbing. I was going to be an athlete! I first tried out for the school basketball team in the 5th grade where the coach, Mrs. Stites, would give us some pretty good advice but who never really covered the basics or the big picture. Or maybe she did, it's quite possible I just wasn't paying attention. Whatever it was though, I never really understood much beyond bouncing the ball around and trying to throw it at the basket, though I only made one basket that year. For the other team.

In the 6th grade Mr. Hanlon, the PE teacher was our coach. Once again I was appropriately placed on the B team where I bumbled around trying to just figure out how to play the game. I remember Mr. Hanlon yelling out the word screen a lot, but I never knew what the heck he was talking about. All I knew is eventually some girl would come up and get into my personal space and make me feel very uncomfortable so I would give her the ball just to get her out of my face. I was also told frequently to be aggressive. Yeah right, like I'm going to actually push or be rude to someone.

Needless to say, I continued to make the B team, but for some reason I also continued to try to play. Why? I did not like playing, I always hoped the coach would just forget me and leave me on the bench. So why did I persist in trying out for the team? I just thought that's what I needed to do, this was where my friends were. Playing sports was the cool thing to do, so I was going to play, by God.

The Walla Walla High School Basketball Team, 1912 and 1913.

Finally in the 9th grade a coach seemed to recognize my talent for participating without actually having to play basketball. Mr. Struefurt asked me to be the statistician of the boys basketball team. He probably couldn't figure out why someone with my ability was still slogging around trying to be on the basketball team at a really big, really sports-oriented school. My only hope was the bench. But somehow this coach saw some value in the kid who wants to watch the game and ride the bus and be a part of the team....but who can't make a basket.

I loved being the statistician! I got to do what I do best, carefully take notes and analyze information while also getting to be part of the action. I enjoyed riding the bus, though I was a little shy of the boys. I enjoyed getting to finally understand the sport in a way that let me be a part of the conversation. And I really enjoyed not having to worry that the coach might make me run out there and play. Now I didn't have to think about anyone trying to take the ball from me or get mad at me. I could watch and participate all from the safety of my established place in the statisticians box. I had a place.

And a place was all I really wanted. In fact, isn't that all any of us want? Just to belong? Not to be a useless nobody on the periphery but an actual important element in the giant machine we call society? Everybody has their own comfort level, their own aspirations, but for me I like to feel like I matter to a group. I've never been content to just observe and follow. I don't really care to be a spectator or merely part of the audience, I want to participate. In everything. I don't want to go to the play, I want to be in the play. I don't want to go to the basketball game, I want to participate in the basketball game. I don't want to quietly listen to other people talk, I want to join in. I don't have to be the star, in fact I don't want to be, I just want a role. It can minor. It just has to have some worth and some thought behind it and I'm happy.

I always kind of envied the people who seem content just to watch, who never want to volunteer, who are fine sitting in the back, who would rather not play or be in the event. What must it be like to not want to get the role or the spot on the team? Does none of that drive to fit in even exist? Or does it come out in other ways? Like with what you wear or who says hi to you?

But that's why family is so important, because whatever your role, you belong.   Not everyone gets lucky with their family, and that's understandable, it is luck of the draw.   And for me, not all of my family is totally awesome. I have cousins I rarely see and have very little in common with, I have family members that I'm not as close to as others. In fact, a thin thread hangs keeping us intact and loving and I sometimes wonder about people with family structures that aren't as connected as mine and I give thanks that today I have my people.

Balloon Stampede

Even though Walla Walla may not have been much of a tourist destination when I was growing up, it still had some fun events. One of my favorites was The Balloon Stampede, a family-friendly event with something for everyone. Held Mother's Day weekend, the event started out nearly 40 years ago with just a few pilots in a field. My Aunt Cindy's dad, Bill Lloyd and his friend Nat Vale organized the first event and it has now grown to one of our biggest local activities.

The event has had many locations since that first fateful field. When I was a child the Balloon Stampede was held at Walla Walla High School. The night glow, though very crowded, was absolutely beautiful over the creek running through the school. The high school location made the event local and friendly, though with few booths and not many balloons. Later the Balloon Stamped moved to Howard Tietan Park. This was my favorite spot for a few reasons. It felt like the perfect size – not crowded, but also cozily occupied. The trees kept everything shady and the open space nearby made every aspect visible. I may have a special place in my heart for the Tietan location because my Uncle Jerry and Aunt Elva had a Funnel Cake booth at that time. We all helped out how we could; being part of the inner workings was really exciting. I remember taking my younger brother, Daniel, when he was about three years old. He was mainly interested in the restored cars on display at the edge of the park and the playground equipment in the middle of the festivities. This worked well for me, since my main occupation is usually watching people and eating – two activities that work fine while babysitting.

A few years after this the Balloon Stamped moved to the Fair Grounds for a few years. While it was there I missed the familiarity and friendliness of Tietan Park, but the Fair Grounds did allow for a more comprehensive event with different musical groups, a huge variety of food and craft booths, and even rides. And of course the balloons, the whole reason for the event, were able to congregate in large groups at the Fair Grounds. But I didn't really spend much time there, call me old-fashioned, but I just missed the homey comfort of a smaller Balloon Stampede. Sometimes things just get too popular and it seems to suck some of the soul away. While at the Fair Grounds the Balloon Stampede was more about the rides than the balloons, or as a friend of mine put it, it's like the fair without the fair.

Now the Balloon Stampede is in a transition with discussion about changing not only the location but even the Mother's Day weekend date. But I can still enjoy my favorite part of the Balloon Stampede: taking my children to the Garrison Middle School field at 5-o'clock in the morning to see all the balloons lift off. Not only is it exciting to watch balloons fill up from very close, seeing the sky fill with dozens of colorful balloons with the occasional roar and flash of fire is breathtaking. And if you oversleep, you may have the luck to be woken by a balloon flying overhead. You will know by the sound of the burner releasing propane, a mysterious sound reminiscent of thunder.

Our dogs used to get so nervous of the thunder roar of the early morning balloons we wouldn't even have to set an alarm. The dogs would come racing into the bedroom to wake us long before we could hear anything, panting nervously. Blue would try to hide under the bed, even though he didn't fit. My dad's dog Snickers would bolt, going who knows where to escape the terror that filled the sky. I know a few people who's dogs get so scared of the balloons that they give the dogs tranquilizers, just like for the 4th of July. But for the rest of us the roar of the fire is a welcome sound, signaling us to run outside and look up at the spring sky filled with color.

Games

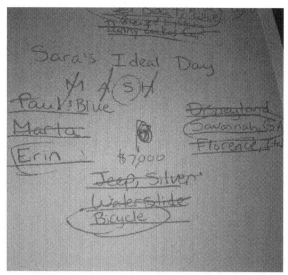

MASH: Who doesn't love this game?

My family and I have always loved playing games. As a child we played games for special occasions, like Christmas and Thanksgiving, but also just as part of our daily lives. My dad taught me to play

Cribbage when I was 10 or 11 and it was our time we spent together, even to this day he will ask me to play a game with him whenever we have a chance. I enjoy this time, it is special to just quietly play, share something fun without any particular goal other than to just have fun.

Our holiday family games, though, are a lot bigger deal. With both my mom's and my dad's family we play Spoons, a very simple card game where everyone tries to get three of a kind as quickly as possible but where the main goal is to grab a spoon before everyone else. The catch is that, like in musical chairs, there is always one less spoon than people, so when that first person gets their three of a kind there is a mad scramble for everyone else to snatch up the spoons. My dad and his brothers are much more inclined to play serious games like Pinochle or Hearts, but those of us that would rather be silly will play Spoons at the other end of the table. Luckily they aren't too particular about our loud noise (I suspect they may turn their hearing aids off about the time we start to play) so the two games at one large table aren't too much of a problem.

My mom's family is always much more exuberant and raucous about any endeavor they take on, it may simply have to do with the fact that instead of being very male-dominated, my mom's family is full of girls. Something about loud girl voices really trumps boy voices. Spoons is a great example of this. A few years ago, everyone was playing spoons at my aunt Janet's when the game just got out of hand. One of my Alexenko cousins, sorry guys it's hard to tell which one of you it was so I'll just blame you all, got a little over-enthusiastic when reaching for the last spoon and....let's just say Janet ended up having to buy a new dining room table. It pretty much epitomized how we play games there.

We also love playing board games, we have had some really great evenings playing Apples to Apples, Scattergories, and Balderdash. We recently went on a family sledding trip and my cousin Chad brought this new game called Loaded Question where we had to reveal truths about ourselves and then guess who's truth it was. A few of us stayed up so late that night that the rest of the family (including the little kids) were a little annoyed with us. The next game I'm going to try out is called 'Cards Against Humanity, I've had a few people tell me how much fun it is. This kept coming up at a recent dinner party when the only game we could find was Trivial Pursuit. I remember loving Trivial Pursuit back in the late 1980's we played it all the time, but the lapse of nearly 30 years has rendered Trivial Pursuit nearly useless at this point. None of us could answer any of the questions, how are we supposed to know who the Olympic winner was for skiing in 1984? How do we know who won best supporting actor for a movie none of us have ever heard of?

With my kids I love playing games, and thank goodness we don't have to play Shoots and Ladders and Candyland anymore (good games, I promise! Just not very interesting), now we are playing games like Clue and Monopoly. More recently, our friend Cindy got us a game Obstacles that we love. It has no rules, just cards with pictures of obstacles (like lava or a lion) to getting home and other cards with these totally random solutions like an umbrella or an ice cube. Everyone has to explain which card they would use and why. That's it. Being a Spanish teacher, I always do mine in Spanish, but the simplicity of the game is what makes it so fun. It reminds me of Apples to Apples in that it's just a fun way to connect without any right or wrong answers. My kids and I love it.

Bikes

Bicycles preparing for a Bad A Bicycle Ride

I'm so lucky I live in Walla Walla because bicycles are my favorite form of transportation. My dad, Greg, was always a bicycle enthusiast. In 2012 he and my godfather, Randy Rogers, spent the summer riding their bicycles across the United States. His blog, 2guysbiketrip.com, is full of interesting photos and information. His latest project is a bicycle-propelled food cart, Panada Bike Bites, where he will sell empanadas at the Saturday Market.

Because of his love for bicycles, my family and I have always been the lucky recipients of his expertise. My first bicycle was a little red banana-seat bicycle with cool plastic strings hanging out of the handle-bars. My older brother, Christian, enjoyed BMX racing at Fort Walla Walla, so he and my dad worked together to make my bike a BMX bike. They replaced the long cushiony seat with a small blue plastic seat, the back-pedal brakes with handbrakes, and the pom-pom handle bars with grippy blue ones. My bike was now a tiny BMX bike, the envy of older boys at school.

At first I wasn't so sure, I was attached to the girly look of the original bike. But after riding my speedy new racing bike I was a convert. I loved that bike! Today I ride a 20-year-old Cannondale mountain bike which I like to refer to as my Faithful Steed because it has carried me to high school, to college classes, to work, over 11 Portland Bridges, throughout Walla Walla, and on many country rides. I have modified this bike in ways similar to my first bicycle, though kind of in the opposite direction. When I was pregnant I rode my bike everywhere (much to people's horror). Because of my added – uh – girth, I needed a more comfortable seat. I replaced my little seat with one called the 'Chubby Buns' seat; what an improvement! Though it is no longer necessary, I still have it because it is so much more comfortable than the original. I have also added a basket and a rack to hold kid seats or panniers.

My dad has always made sure my children could ride bicycles, too. When they were very young I had them on a 'CoPilot' bike seat mounted to the back of my bike. As they got older they both fit into a Burley Bike Trailer, though there were times when they would bicker back there, kind of like a roving fight. I really miss those days. Now they both ride their own bikes, an exciting transformation that gives them a new freedom that I am still getting used to. The past seven summers my family and I have participated in the Portland Bridge Pedal, a 14-mile bike ride criss-crossing bridges of Portland's downtown. It is very family friendly and my children love it. When she was 8, Natalie rode on her own bike, rather than attached behind someone else, she was thrilled. My son rode on the tagalong behind me and he loved being up high rather than in a bike seat. The next year they both got to ride their own bikes. Noah, though, really struggled to keep up on his teeny-tiny bicycle, and since we were in one of the last groups to start we ended up finishing last. Last. In a race of 20,000 people, we were so far behind that the police were driving slooooowly behind us with their lights flashing. They asked me if I could make Noah go faster so they could open I-5, but they they realized this was futile considering he was six and working his tail off. So the city of Portland had to wait for Noah. Despite finishing last, he was so proud of himself for completing the race. The Bridge Pedal has become an important family tradition that we all look forward to each summer.

My dad recently arrived at my house rocking his new electric bicycle. He had it specially made in Portland and had just gotten home that very afternoon and was proudly buzzing all over town to show it off. The fact that it was January and 30 degrees did not faze my dad at all, he kindly offered to let me try it out, though seeing that I was wearing slippers and had left the comfort of my fireplace to come shivering out to admire it, I was forced to decline. As his body has gotten a little further on in years, my dad has been struggling a bit with his hips, making biking harder. This electric bicycle would now allow him to continue riding as he always had, but without such strain on his joints. I'm so thankful my dad is looking for ways to stay active.

Walla Walla is a beautiful place to ride bikes. Our relatively flat topography, tree-lined streets and quiet roads make biking feasible and pleasant nearly year-round. One of my favorite rides is the Bad Ass Bicycle Ride, organized by Andy Alexander and Stacy Buchanan. We meet every month or so for a group ride that has a faint spark of civil disobedience to it. The organizers often choose a theme so we can dress up and bring noise-makers to really make for a festive event. There is a hippie ride, a Halloween ride, and my favorite, the Tweed Ride. The

Tweed Ride gives people a chance to wear their old-fashioned tweedy finery while riding through town in a loud mob, a nice dichotomy. My kids love participating in this event, especially now that they can ride their own bikes and don't have to be dragged behind in a bike trailer.

Sara and Sandra on the Tweed Ride

Of course, one of the best ways to ride a bicycle in Walla Walla is out on our beautiful country roads. As a driver I get pretty nervous passing bikes out by the wheat fields, there is no shoulder and they can be hard to see. It is dangerous to ride out there and the cyclist needs to take responsibility to look out for cars. One of my colleagues was hit and killed riding out in the country, and it is still something we mourn. But the beautiful countryside continues to beckon, despite the danger. Being out in the wheat fields overlooking the valley with the mountains in the distance is soothing and lovely, I feel so lucky to live in a place where I can do this.

Bikes have always been popular in Walla Walla

Cruisin' the Gut

Who doesn't love cruisin' the gut?

As a kid, Walla Walla didn't have a lot going on, the downtown was full of vacant buildings and the newly constructed mall never really took off. One of the funnest things for people to do was cruise the gut. Ah, cruising the gut, driving up and down where the only aim was to socialize. I wish I had gotten to, the closest I ever got was when I went to a slumber party at my friend Tracy's house in junior high and her sweet mom took us. We had so much fun driving back and forth from Albertsons all the way down Isaacs and Rose to Safeway! We even got brave and had her honk at a few older guys. We thought we were so cool. By the time I had my driver's license a few years later, though, there really wasn't much action in the cruising arena – not unless you count cowboys showing off their big trucks in the Albertson's parking lot. Or the EuroCar CreationZ guys comparing their tricked out cars in the Penguin parking lot.

But I've heard tales of Cruising in the 60's, the apparent hey-day of cruising when the streets were full of young people all through downtown. Where you could honk at your friends or future friends, or where one misplaced honk of the horn could get the wrong car-load to stop. Where people could congregate in parking lots and street corners, their cars full of friends and even beer – I guess D.U.I. laws weren't as harsh in these days. An idea my Fafa loved to wax nostalgic about, he would sigh and shake his head at the oppression of today's government. "Ah," he would lament, "we could drink too much at the bar and drive home without any worry. If the police pulled us over and saw we were drunk they would just drive in front of us to make sure we had someone to follow." God bless him, I sure do miss that Leonard Mobley.

But back to those wild teens from the past, B.A.ing in the 1950's and 1960's, streaking in the 1970's. I can't let my uncle Tom Alexenko off the hook. Now, admittedly, Tom is still pretty wild! But apparently I missed out on some really good nights before I was born, because everyone loves to tell of Tom's streaking escapades, especially the time he streaked from The Green to Pepe's Pizza. I guess Tom really enjoyed streaking, no problem for someone who is thin and fast (and probably drunk). He planned ahead and gave my dad his clothes to take to the bathroom across the street at Pepe's, then he raced from the bathroom at The Green, through the bar, into the street – where he jumped up and clicked his heels together like a leprechaun before running into the pizza parlor. As everyone reminisced about the event at a recent family dinner, there was a lot of discussion about whether or not he was barefoot or wearing boots. I remember the old bathroom at the Green before they remodeled and I can't imagine being barefoot in there, not to mention running on pavement, but − hey, who knows, he could have been barefoot.

Today, no one cruises the gut. We have to call a taxi or walk when we drink too much. And, saddest by far, I've never seen a streaker, in fact as I write this the word streaker comes up on spell check as not a word. My poor generation. We'd get arrested if we tried to do half the things our parents laugh about getting away with. But at least we could probably all beat the pants off them at Super Mario Bros. Yep.

Fiat

When I was in college I had the privilege of driving a 1976 Fiat Spider. Red, convertible, soft-top, leather interior. Are you thinking, what a spoiled brat? Yes, it may have appeared that way – though the reality was no one else in the family wanted to drive this temperamental beauty so I was stuck with it. Believe me, I would have preferred the family Subaru or even the Volkswagen Van…. But I was the youngest driver and got the left-overs.

The Fiat probably started out as an amazing vehicle, but by the time I got to drive it in 1992 it was just plain difficult. For one thing nothing ever seemed to stay where it was supposed to; every time I accelerated the rear-view mirror would pop out, the stereo would fall out, and the glove compartment slid to the floor of the passenger seat. I got pretty adept at catching all of these – though if I also happened to be turning left at the same time, my driver-side door would fly open. Added to this fun, the engine would die if I ever came to a complete stop. I usually tried to avoid this by steering clear of stoplights and crawling through stop signs, but I often had to rely on passengers to jump out and push while I popped the clutch to start the car. Luckily, as a teenager I never had a shortage of passengers.

My older brother Christian didn't fare any better when my parents loaned out cars. He was allowed to use my dad's green Volkswagen Van. Though the van was pretty solid structurally it did have other minor issues like no heat, brakes that suddenly disappeared, and a stick-shift that was nearly impossible to get into reverse. More importantly, though, some previous owner had written a large 'Nuke the Whales' on the bumper. Eventually my dad grew tired of strangers' anger (or their lack of humor?) and he painted over the 'Nuke' part of the declaration. So for awhile the bumper just read '_____ the Whales'. Later, when Chris got to use the van, he was going through a very outspoken born-again Christian phase. He put a 'Jesus Saves' sticker over the crossed out 'Nuke' so now the bumper read 'Jesus Saves the Whales'. I'm not sure if this was an improvement.

I suppose it is necessary for teenagers to drive difficult cars so they don't get too satisfied with themselves and also to help them appreciate their better cars as adults. Oh, yes, and maybe because most teens can't afford to buy their own really nice car. My boyfriend in high school, Pablo, rode a skateboard, which was very cool and also pretty practical – not to mention a whole lot cheaper than a car. Most of my friends rode bicycles, as did I when the Fiat was not working or someone else wanted to drive it. Now I drive a big, comfortable Toyota – perfect for car seats, backpacks, groceries and other miscellaneous items that seem to accumulate in cars. My Fiat days have made me appreciate a car that has heated seats, always starts and consistently stays in one piece. Now maybe I should get a bumper sticker.

Telephones

My dad and step-mom recently gave us a rotary-dial phone. My kids were so intrigued by this object of mystery that they spent the afternoon dialing all of the relatives I would allow them to call. Who knew this could be so fun?

When I was a kid that is all we had, a big phone with the cord attached with a dial in the middle that took a long time to dial. If you got impatient and tried to spin the rotary too fast it would dial the wrong number. If it sat outside, like the phone on my grandparents' patio, dirt would get under the dial making a clean streak where your finger traced a line in the dirt. Eventually everyone had the push-button dialer, though the telephone cord hung on for a long time, allowing any family member within earshot to hear anything that was being said. At our house we only had one phone, it was in the kitchen. It was mortifying for me to receive a phone call from a boy when I was in high school because, even though they pretended not to, my whole family could hear everything I said. The only way to have a private conversation was to pull the phone into a closet and whisper. Now texting allows people to have private conversations whenever they want.

Cell phones aren't easy for people, especially my grandma's generation. My godmother Connie tried to give her mom Martha a cell phone a couple of years before Martha passed away. My Great-Aunt Martha was so sweet and really smart, but when it came to mastering the cell phone she was just lost. Even though this phone they got her was very simple and designed with a more advanced-aged user in mind with few, larger buttons, Martha never really did get the hang of it. That Christmas morning when she first received the phone, Connie's friend Nancy decided to call Martha so we could all help her out. The three ladies were sitting on the couch, Martha on one end, Connie in the middle, and Nancy on the other end. Nancy dialed Martha's new phone and it began to ring. With all of us shouting at her to press the great big green button Martha got a little flustered, but she managed to answer her new phone.

"Hello?" She asked.

"Hello, Martha?" Responded Nancy, sitting less than two feet away in the same room.

"Who is this?" Asked Martha.

Martha never really did catch on to the new cell phone. My Grandma Esther, who we called Gram, had about the same amount of success. Just getting the thing turned on was too much trouble. My dad would go and help her and remind her of how to use it, but she wasn't that interested. Just getting her to talk to our answering machines was enough new technology for her. I loved when she left me messages, she didn't leave the message as if she was talking to me, she always addressed the machine, as in, "Machine, will you please tell Sara that I am calling her and that she should call me back?"

My other grandma, Nanny, is just a few years younger and has no trouble with the answering machine but has no interest in cell phones either. She makes all of us laugh, though, whenever we talk about emails or text messages she kind of harrumphs and asks why she didn't get the email or the text? Never mind that she doesn't have a way to get them, she would at least like to receive these messages. I'll try to remember to print them out for her.

But mastering technology is not an age issue, it was my dad was who got me involved with texting. Back in 2004 or so I had not really heard of text messaging, in fact I don't think I started really texting regularly until about 2008. But it was my dad who kept insisting I try this amazing new technology. I didn't understand the point, he kept sending me texts and I would call him back. He would laugh and tell me to text him back. At first it just seemed like a pain, why bother typing it in when you can call the person and clarify everything? But eventually I started to catch on, and now I almost prefer text messages, though for really chatting or catching up I still like the phone.

It was a completely different experience to talk on the phone 25 years ago. For one thing, a person had to call your house and whoever answered the phone got to talk to them. I LOVED answering the phone when I was little, even though it was rarely for me. I loved getting to say hello to whoever was at the other end. As an older child and teenager I didn't like this quite so much. Having to greet various parents and siblings could get tricky and embarrassing, especially when calling a boy or a new friend. Or an extra helpful parent. My dear friend, Erin's dad was one of those parents. Dr. Johnson felt it was his duty to teach me manners. If I would call and say, "Is Erin there?" he would simply respond, "Yes...", and wait for me to politely ask to speak to her. MAY I speak to her, of course, not CAN I speak to her. Now I appreciate his etiquette lesson, but for a second grader all of this seemed so complicated.

It was also fun to tease people about how people in their family answered the phone. Now, with a cell phone, it is usually pretty clear who is calling, it is obviously our own phone, so when we answer most people now give a variation of saying their own name or even just launching in to a conversation. But when I was a kid I had a few friends with parents who had more creative methods than the traditional, "hello?" My friend Elaine's mom, Joyce, answered with a cheerful "YELL-oh!" which we, to this day, still imitate whenever we see Elaine. My colleague, Kristin, said her parents forced her to answer the phone "Gehrett residence!" giving her friends plenty of fodder for teasing. My aunt Florene would sometimes answer the phone with appropriate expressions like "Good afternoon!" or "Merry Christmas!" which I always enjoyed.

And speaking of my Aunt Florene, this reminds me of the wrong number phone calls – which used to happen a lot to us because we lived on the same street as Florene and my Uncle Barry. My cousin Chad (the handsome UPS man) used to get SO many phone calls at our house from girls. I still have their now-useless phone number memorized because I had to always redirect them to the correct number. In fact, I have a lot of old phone numbers memorized, none of which would get a hold of anyone I know today. My mom said when she was a kid all the numbers in Walla Walla started with JA (like 5-2) and everyone would say their number was JAckson-whatever the rest of the number was. I don't have any numbers memorized now; I might be in trouble if I ever lost my cell phone!

The art of having conversations with strangers may also now be lost. In fact, people today (I'll admit even I do this) don't just get to avoid phone conversations with friends' families, but can even avoid seeing them when they go to a friend's house. It is so much easier to just text, I'm here! than to walk to the front door, say hi to mom or dad, and have to make small talk. In fact – do people younger than me even know what small talk is? People raised in the age of cell phones, texting, and email may not have this skill. I wonder how this will affect our world in the long run? But at the same time, people raised without computers might not know how to Skype or IM, so maybe we'll all balance each other out. And the most important thing – at least we are all still communicating!

At least phones no longer need a switchboard like in 1957...or do they?

Maybe this is what nanobots are doing inside our cellphones today.

Neighborhood

I was lucky to have my Aunt Florene live just down the street from me. She, my Uncle Barry, and my cousins Chad and Kim lived only three houses down on the same street. When our parents bought these houses it wasn't considered a popular choice to buy an old house near the center of town. In the 1970's people in Walla Walla wanted to live out in the newly forming suburbs, ironically in the very farmland my grandparents were no longer farming but couldn't afford to pass on to their children. The newly built ranch-style homes were attracting people with money so the working class people like my parents, the bakers and grave-diggers and cannery workers, were buying the more run-down houses in town. Our house was $40,000 in 1976 and needed some work. In 2014 it is worth about $300,000 and is in what is considered to be one of the nicest neighborhoods in town. But hindsight is 20/20 and no one suspected that the old houses would be so valuable someday.

We had tons of little kids running all over the neighborhood, though most were boys just a little bit older than me. I'm not sure what happened around 1972 but there was an explosion of boys in our neighborhood around that time. By the time I came around in 1976 there was only Elaine who lived in the big white house behind us, we were the only girls on the block unless you counted my cousin Kim who was eight years older. Those boys had so much fun riding big wheels and later bicycles all over the place, Elaine and I would try to keep up with them, but it was futile. They would also play hide-and-seek and kick-the-can, which we did get to join in. I loved those games! Even later, as an early teenager, my friends and I would play hide-and-seek outside our houses. Although our favorite was Ghost in the Graveyard and we play it to this day.

Ghost in the Graveyard isn't quite as well known as other outdoor hiding games, but it's similar to sardines or kick the can, although it is always played after dark. One person hides and everyone else counts from the porch (one-o-clock, two-o-clock). Once the counters reach midnight they set off clockwise around the house to look for the ghost. Once spotted, the ghost is free to tag someone as we all race to the porch, but the hard part is is no one but the ghost can turn around and run counter clockwise.

It could get confusing having so many Van Donges on the same street. We never got our mail confused, though, because my Uncle Barry worked for the Post Office, but like I said, we did get phone calls for cousin Chad a lot. Chad was (and still is) that guy. That guy. Handsome and friendly, loves talking to people, remembers everyones name, good at sports. Chad and my older brother Christian were in the same grade at school and were good friends, but where Chris was quiet Chad was talkative, where Chris was careful Chad was bold, where Chris was uncertain Chad was confident. Thankfully Chris was also generous and didn't long for the spotlight so it never seemed to bother him that Chad got so much attention. It may have been good for both of them that the world-renowned football star Drew Bledsoe was also in their class all through elementary school too. That'll keep you humble.

But by the time they were in the fifth grade girls started calling Chad. About three times a week the phone would ring, I would lunge for it (why? Who calls a first grader? Oh well, answering the phone is fun) and it would be a giggling girl, or two on an extension. And I'd give them Chad's phone number. After my own and my Nanny and Fafa's phone number, Chad's family was the next number I memorized.

I myself attempted calling boys a few times with my friends, it never really went as well as I hoped it would. We would usually plan for it for days, deciding what to say, practicing, one of us being the boy while the other went through our lines. We would often write down what we were going to say. Unfortunately we never realized that elementary-aged boys are just simply not interested in girls. They are interested in sports and matchbox cars and dinosaurs. But not girls. So when we would call they would inevitably ask us something terribly hurtful like why were we calling? Or was there something we needed? Oh! The agony of it!

Having my family just down the street had some really good benefits too, number one being that if I got locked out of the house I could always run down to their house for the key and get in. For some reason we always locked our house and they never locked theirs. Maybe it was that my stepmom, Suzanne, had grown up in San Diego and just couldn't trust that Walla Walla could be so safe that you wouldn't need to lock the house. But I was supposed to carry a key and let myself in if no one was home. Of course, being who I am, I couldn't keep track of anything, especially not something as small as a key and it seemed I often got home from school and the door was locked. So my solution was always to run down the alley to Barry and Florene's for the spare key. They were the sort to not only leave the house unlocked but the door open, the lights on, and the TV blaring whether or not they were home. Or they may have been home, who knows. It was pretty low-key over there.

I enjoyed spending time with my Aunt Florene, she is really mellow and patient. She was a teacher and taught all different age-levels from pre-school all the way up through adults getting their GED. When I was in my early teens she taught me how to bake bread and I am still so thankful to her for it. I would go to her house after school and we made different types, plain white, sourdough, oatmeal. When she had deemed me good enough to not need lessons anymore she gave me this fabulous wooden bowl and my own bread cookbook, both of which I still use today to make bread.

When I was in my mid-twenties I attempted to leave my husband one time before I was able to successfully get away. I stayed with Florene for a few weeks and it was so wonderful to get to talk to her and spend time with her as an adult. Florene had moved to Walla Walla as a young adult when she married my Uncle Barry, but she grew up in Parsons Kansas. I always thought it was so cute that her sisters were named Marlene and Darlene. Marlene, Darlene, and Florene. Plus they have a brother named Herman. I am so thankful I was lucky enough to have her and the rest of my family down the block.

The Van Donge Family enjoys being together: Dean, Florene, Greg, Dave, and Bob

Swimming in Walla Walla - Yesterday and Today

"What was your favorite childhood activity?" I asked my mom, Linda. Of course I already knew what the answer would be: The Nat. I've heard her and my aunts rhapsodizing about the D. M. Smith Natatorium my whole life. The dances. The pool. How all the kids in town would go there to meet up with friends. My dad, Greg was more partial to Graybill's, which was on the South side of town near their farm. My mom laughed and said Graybill's was a swamp, but the Van Donge kids all enjoyed swimming in a natural pond.

When I was a child, my friends and I met at Memorial, a private pool near Borleske Stadium. The high dive and slide made it a place to be daring, but the frozen Charleston Chews were my biggest motivator for going. Today my kids, Natalie and Noah, get a lot of use out of a tiny round plastic pool – surprisingly fun, but combined with washing my car, the sprinkler, and an occasional squirt gun we make the most of our summer days at home. If we need to swim, we could go to the YMCA and they have taken quite a few swim lessons there. But nothing beats an outdoor pool, which Walla Walla doesn't currently have. Don't get anyone started on the subject, it is a political land mine.

When I was growing up my grandparents had a swimming pool. I practically lived at their house during the summer and I swam so often that my family called me Swimming Sara. I also swam so much that my blonde hair turned a kind of mermaid-y green, but I was too young to really care. My cousins and I would entertain ourselves for hours pretending to have olympics and creating all sorts of tricks and dives and synchronized swimming events. But even though we had a swimming pool, we always ended up at the nearby creek. My grandparents lived near Garrison Creek running through a beautiful wooded area right in the middle of town. My brother and cousins and I spent much of our childhood playing in and around the creek there. We watched water skippers, caught and released crawdads, and floated plants down the slow creek. My cousin, Skyler, caught cans full of snakes – scaring the rest of us in his innocent eagerness to show them off. We would float twigs and flowers down the stream and race them to see if we could beat the water. We built ourselves beaver dens and forts under the nearby trees. We walked through the thickets of pussy willows and cat-tails. It wasn't that long ago, but my heart aches to go there again.

Recently a developer managed to get ahold of this beautiful land and build a small housing development. I can barely drive past now without crying as I see the creek stripped back to a small trickle, the trees cut down, and cement poured nearly up to the edge. This past summer I brought my own children a block west to play in the same creek behind Pioneer Middle School, but a woman walking past told us children aren't allowed to play near the creek, it can destroy it. Somehow I think small children poking sticks in the mud must be less damaging than bulldozers and cement....but we vacated the area, returning to the blue plastic pool in our backyard.

My little story is nothing, absolutely nothing compared to the stories so many others could tell. I have trouble not going on and on about the area west of Walla Walla where three rivers meet up. A few years ago one of my colleagues arranged to have a Native American man speak to our 8th graders and he told a poignant account of how The Snake, The Columbia, and The Walla Walla Rivers all used to come together in a beautiful area. For millennia Native people would meet there for a giant potlatch at the time when the cherries blossomed. Every spring all the tribes would peacefully meet to trade goods, fish, and celebrate the arrival of spring. Now the Columbia is dammed and there is a pulp mill there, a paper factory that stinks so badly you have to roll up the windows when you drive by; my cousins that live nearby only drink bottled water. Though I love hydroelectric power and paper, I still get sad when I drive by, I just think about how my heart aches for my own little river spot, now gone, and I think of all the people who must have watched that one disappear too. SMH.

Graybill's Pool

The Nat, circa 1950

School Dances

Do you remember school dances? If you are anything like me, of course you do. Who can forget the terror of standing in a dark gym, clumped together with friends, hoping some boy will come over and ask you to dance? Though, in retrospect, how could a boy possibly be that brave? When my friends and I were in 9th grade at Wa-Hi, we all decided we were going to go to the Homecoming dance. We picked out our unsuspecting victims, oops, I mean boys, and told their friends to have them ask us. Yes, this is how girls operate when faced with a desperate situation. Poor Jason was my target; he was kind and available, so good enough qualifications for me. After arranging for him to ask me to the dance my friends and I were eating lunch outside by the creek and he approached our circle. I was terrified when he asked if he could talk to me. I was terrified. Leave it to egotistical ninth grade me to give no thought to how this poor guy must have felt walking up to a dozen ninth grade girls alone, I was just thinking of my own racing heart and ringing ears. All I could squeak out was a, "Wait! Ask me later!" to which he nodded and started backing away. Suddenly, I was surrounded by a frantic group of ninth boys, who had been nearby watching Jason. They were all talking at once, asking me what I was doing. I remember in particular a guy named Kevin was really upset. I guess he had been watching Jason, preparing to ask his own potential date to the dance. I realized then that this was a big deal, me not being cool and just saying, "Sure, I'll go with you to the dance!" made all these other boys even more nervous. Ugh. I still feel sorry to this day. Luckily it all worked out, Jason called me that afternoon and asked me in a safer setting, over the phone. We went to the dance together (an awkward experience, I simply was too young to date) and I was able to check Homecoming off my list.

High School dances are kind of a blur to me, and no, I definitely was not one of those kids who snuck in drunk. I think it was just the loud music and swirling lights and crowds all created an experience that was overwhelming for a more reserved student like me. I appreciated the dance instructions Mrs. Pam Thompson and the other P.E. teachers gave us. And my ballet and jazz dance instruction from Idalee Hutson-Fish and Kathy Halfacre gave me the ability to move to the music, though not necessarily the confidence to do it in front of my classmates.

I spent a few years chaperoning dances at Garrison Middle School. It was a lot like I (vaguely) remember, though there were no slow dances at Garrison. Remember those??? The music would change and maybe, just maybe a boy would come over (i.e. get up the nerve) and ask one of us to dance. Usually they came in groups and asked us. I can tell you every slow dance I ever danced at Pioneer, a testament to either A) my popularity or B) how important they were. The funny thing about the slow dance besides how much emphasis we put on them was how extremely awkward they were once you actually got yourself into the situation. The boy, arms stiffly resting on the girls shoulders. The girl, awkwardly holding his sides. Neither really making eye contact, turning in a clockwise circle making small talk. Did I say this was awkward? Oh yes, twice already. Maybe this is why we don't have slow dances at Garrison now. I interviewed some eighth graders about our dances and they all mentioned that there are two slow dances at Pioneer, and all seemed relieved they don't have to worry about slow dances here. As usual I had trouble getting serious answers from the boys. Once boy said he goes, for sure. He twerks. Another said he dances with all the ladies. I do believe both of these boys were teasing. Another said, yes, he goes, and he even dances sometimes. But no way would he ever slow dance. No way. Two girls said they might go in for a minute, but they don't dance, no one really does. Ah, yes, leave it to 8th grade girls to be honest.

At our most recent dance I danced so much I woke up the next day sore. I arrived in the middle of the first song, the dark gym was crowded with nervous kids hunched uncomfortably in clumps. I marched to the front of the gym and stood in front of the music system in a small patch of light and began to dance. Immediately a buzz went through the crowd, someone's dancing! Everyone crept closer to see who this brave soul could be, who could be so confident as to dance? At a dance? The was a heave of recognition and relief and slight disappointment when they realized, oh it's just Ms. Van Donge. Of course she'll dance.

But they were intrigued and all eyes were on me as I simply stepped back and forth to the music, occasionally raising my hands to shoulder height. I kept it purposefully simple because my goal as a 16 year veteran teacher was to get this party started and I knew it wouldn't take long for these kids to start copying my movements if they weren't too complex. Sure enough, within moments a couple of brave boys (who were probably desperate to move to the music) jumped in line behind me and began copying everything I did. This opened the floodgates, within two minutes at least forty kids were lined up behind me copying my dance moves. I stepped to the right and pointed my arm disco-style to the side? 40 middle schoolers stepped to the right and pointed their arms disco-style to the side. Pretty cute, really. Those kids and I were twisting, shuffling, getting our eagle on, and shaken' it like a Polaroid picture. By the end of the second song I had to stop to catch my breath, but I spent the better part of an hour dancing my tail off and I could feel it for the next two days. Did I ever mention I love dancing? I'm not sure if there are many jobs in this world where I can dance, but the three or four times a year I get to dance with a bunch of middle schoolers make my job worth every difficulty.

Once a dancer, always a dancer

Radio

I have always enjoyed listening to the radio. Even though the ads annoy me, the station will eventually fade out on long trips, and I have no control of the music, I still like the variety and surprise of the radio. My daughter also loves the radio, especially the Top-40 stations. It doesn't really matter what the song is, if it is on one of these two stations she will listen and sing along. My son likes show tunes and Christmas music, I'll write about this some other day.

Listening to the radio is not really the same type of experience today as it was in the past. Radio stations seem to be run by strangers who are living in far-away cities. The only local information is the occasional ad or sporting event. KWCW, from Whitman College, has local DJs and relevant local announcements, and KTEL also plays local sporting events and stories about local events, but KTEL is nothing like it was in the past. At a recent family dinner my parents and godparents were reminiscing about the days when hearing rock and roll on the radio was really special. My dad told me real rock and roll music was so hard to seek out when he was in high school that the only time he could even hear it was late at night when the local station would play fifteen minutes of rock music. My Godmother, Connie was quick to add that this music was usually not really very good, just some over-played bubble gum music, not the real rock music they wanted to hear - not, that is until "Rockin' Cochran" came along. Dave Cochran was a Senior at Wa-HI who played really good music, not just top 40: Cream, Hendrix, The Doors. He was also a supporter of local musicians and would promote local concerts. Plus he took requests. Connie told us how she and her friends would at times send subversive messages this way, requesting the Buckinghams "Kind of a Drag" for someone they didn't really like or "Monday, Monday" to bemoan the upcoming school week. Of course there were also the legitimate requests like "Good Day Sunshine" when all was well with the world. Since this was a local station, people could stop in to visit. Dave Cochran or Burl Barer, another DJ (who incidentally is now a best-selling author) would invite them in. Connie acknowledges that being a cute 16-year-old in a mini-skirt may have made the dropping in easier to do! At this time there were also many radio-sponsored contests, made more interesting than the contests of today because everyone had to use rotary-dial phones.

When I was in elementary school we still had a popular local station - KISS 101 FM, located at the top of the Marcus Whitman Hotel. My cousin Chad Van Donge was a DJ in the evenings and I enjoyed not only listening to his show, but also the residual popularity that came from being related to a real, live DJ. Like KTEL in the 1960's, KISS FM took requests and dedications, held contests, and hosted visitors. The dedications, which you could phone in every evening from 9:00 - 10:00, were called "Blowing a Kiss" and it was always exciting for my friends and myself to listen and hope that maybe someone would blow a kiss to us. I remember the day in the late 1980's when KISS FM was suddenly Kiiiiisss Country. Without warning they had changed their format, which at first we thought was a joke, but later proved to be sadly true. This was the end of my radio-listening days. I switched my little clock radio over to OK 95 and tried to enjoy listening to Top-40 from the Tri-Cities, but I missed the camaraderie of having real people here in my own community playing music over the radio. It was about this time that Grunge music started to become popular. My older brother bought a Red Hot Chili Peppers CD (the first CD I had ever seen) and then my cousin Karie gave me a Nirvana CD and my music listening changed. I began enjoying the control I had over music and the lack of ads. I received a Ghetto Blaster for Christmas and with this the ability to make mixed tapes from the CDs. Radio became a thing of the past. Today there are so many ways to hear music: CDs, records, on the internet, iPods, and yes, we still have the good old radio.

Mixed Tapes

To paraphrase Beastie Boys, one of my favorite bands, you need a good mixed tape to get you in the right mood. One of our district technology experts was in my classroom recently, and as he worked his magic creating a Frankenstein-type combination of projector/VHS/speaker so I can show a Spanish-language telenovela (soap opera) to my students, we had a conversation about mixed tapes. He's a young guy, so right after I mentioned tapes and what a pain they were, cuing them or getting tangled up, I realized he might not know what I meant. But he understood and then even mentioned how cool mixed tapes used to be. We reminisced about how much effort it used to take to make a mixed tape, so different from downloading and burning a CD today. Back then you actually had to sit and carefully cue each song, stopping and starting at precisely the right moment. Twice. Once from the original tape then again onto the mixed tape. You had to sift through different tapes, looking for exactly the right song, deciding where it should go on the mixed tape. Plus there was all the effort of labeling and writing down songs. And of course there was always the little note that accompanied the gift of the mixed tape.

A young man give me a mixed tape once, years and years ago. Even though he was actually not a very good boyfriend – one of those who would disappear for days on end with no explanation and who never had money to pay for himself – I swallowed my self-respect long enough to date the guy even though he was a loser. Why? The mixed tape. I went out with him a few times then told him it was over, but he made me a mixed tape that night and presented it the next morning with a love letter. Songs like 'Wish you were here' and 'Being with you is like being stoned' (is that romantic?) were not really that persuasive, it was merely the idea that he had most likely stayed up all night thinking of me making a mixed tape. So I continued to go out with him. Hey, a little effort can go a long way.

I asked some of my students if they knew what a mixed tape was and they seemed surprised I would ask. Of course they know what a mixed tape is. A couple were proud to admit they have even seen a tape deck. Ricky's sister used to have a Nissan with a tape deck in it. Brian even used to OWN a tape deck. Whoa. Then they all went back to the videos they were creating on IPads. I couldn't really get any fourteen year olds to engage in conversation about mixed tapes, so my assumption has to be they probably don't have a lot of experience with the tedious experience of actually making them. And why would they? They have plenty of technology to be absorbed by now, so of course they don't bother with this relic any more than I do. But it's good they are aware that there is a thing that exists called a mixed tape, the generation gap isn't that big yet.

Saturday Night

Anyway, I did grow up fairly unscathed and I did have a lot of fun and goodness mixed in with a normal amount of difficulty. I was kind of a freak about trying to be perfect, maybe as a backlash against what I viewed as a slightly less than perfect childhood compared to all my classmates and friends who had married parents and who only had to live in one home. When I say freak, you may think I mean one of those people who works pretty hard at school and didn't really socialize. But I wasn't just a hard worker, I was a single-minded minion, never stopping, never sleeping, never resting. My mind always racing, racing, racing to get me out and on to better things, though I had friends and made time to socialize too. By the time I was a sophomore in high school I had started spending time with kids who were a little more...maybe we could say interesting. I was starting to lose interest in following the crowd, with participating with what the "popular" kids were doing. I was still friends with these kids and would always remain friendly with them, but by the time I'd gotten adjusted to high school I began to listen to music that was no longer on the radio like The Cure and The Red Hot Chili Peppers plus I'd gotten tired of having people at school make comments about my clothes or hair if they veered from what everyone else was wearing even just a little bit. I started to rebel a little bit against my own classmates.

Oddly enough, I probably rebelled more against the mainstream mentality of my classmates than I did against my parents, mainly because my parents had always encouraged me to be a free thinker. I had never felt comfortable wearing something or doing something or listening to music just because someone else had deemed it cool. In fact, the more the large crowd of my classmates started doing things the more I began going in the opposite direction. I started participating in community theater and writing for the school newspaper, I started wearing mens Levis 501 Jeans. I stopped trying to make my straight blonde hair curly and big. And I started hanging out with Kim, Christine, and other fun girls.

I met Kim because I started dating Pablo, a boy from the DeSales, the Catholic High School. Kim was dating Sean, one of Pablo's good friends, and being the self-actualized women that we weren't, Kim and I were at Whitman College one lovely spring evening to watch our boyfriends skateboard. As happens sometimes when timing is magical, Kim and I became instant friends. As we watched our cute new boyfriends ride around on sandpaper-covered boards with wheels, we chatted about our mutual dislike for Top-40 music (which ironically we both now listen to as we near 40!). By the end of the evening we were exchanging phone numbers and by the end of the school year it was if we had always been friends.

Kim introduced me to her friend Christine. My first impression of her was that she had to be scary and harsh. In truth Christine's aggressive exterior shielded a very shy and gentle personality. It took me no time at all to also become great friends with Christine. The funny thing with the three of us was that both Christine and Kim really subscribed to the whole grunge look but I always maintained my clean-cut good girl image. I couldn't really help it, but I somehow could never bring myself to fully embrace the no-makeup look that was popular in those days. I never really could do anything popular. Even if I wished I didn't have to, somehow I always had to be true to myself, I couldn't do anything false. So I never really fit in anywhere. But with Kim and Christine this didn't matter, they liked me because I was who I was.

Somehow we developed a little band of girls and we really knew how to have fun. Besides Kim and Christine, I also spent a lot of time with

Elaine, Monica, and Berny. One Saturday night in particular stands out for me. Four of us were trying to ride a skateboard, borrowed from a guy who liked Elaine that I secretly called Freaky Mike, to differentiate him from all the other Mike's around. Like Sara, Mike is a very common name for people my age. I was wedged between Monica and Elaine, my eyes tightly clenched shut as I kept a death grip on Monica's shoulders. Berny, who was at the front of the board, ordered us to lift our feet on the count of three. Just as we began gaining momentum down the steepest sidewalk for blocks, I felt Elaine slip from her spot behind me. With a thud, she sat on the cement leaving me on the edge of the board as we began rolling. Never one to allow a moment to be dull, Elaine jumped up and put her hands on my shoulders, giving us a huge shove that sent us barreling down the sidewalk. I could feel the lines of the sidewalk thu-thunking under me, first fast then slowing as we leveled out. Shrieking with exuberant fifteen-year old laughter we piled off the scratchy board, clamoring to ride down the hill again.

Berny, being the only one coordinated enough to maneuver the board while standing up, road back to Elaine's. Elaine's mom, concerned about the morality of her sheltered angel, had reluctantly agreed to allow us to stay the night. Joyce was convinced we were going to expose her innocent daughter to something terrible, refusing to see that it was Elaine, in fact, who was often the instigator. And in fact we did have an ulterior motive on this evening, we were hoping to finally join the world of teenage parties. Elaine had heard from Freaky Mike that there might be a party at a guy named Scott's house.

Although Scott had graduated from high school, he had spent the past year living like he was still in his senior year, minus the responsibility of classes or parents. He rented a two-room apartment in a run down white house on Washington Street, downstairs from my similarly motivated older brother who was in the same post-high school situation. This night was our ticket into the dark and mysterious world of....partying.

You know, parties. Not birthday-cake-and-ice-cream-ice-chalet-movie-theater-momsendinvitations parties. No no no. These parties were the kind of event the whole school discussed on Monday morning in the locker lobby. Dark rooms lit by pretty young girls, giggling to evil sounding music we had trained ourselves to love while older guys feigned interest in some skateboarding magazine or whatever. The activity meant nothing - it was the possibility of actually attending our first real party! With real teenagers! The four of us could barely contain our anticipation.

Of course, Elaine's mom wanted us home by 10:00, on a beautiful spring Saturday when the sun would still be a hint of lighter blue in the night sky. Home by 10:00! Which was actually pretty reasonable, had she not cared the whole novelty of the party scene would have lost at least a small portion of interest for us. So, out till 10:00 we went, racing through the twilight, free! By the time we reached the lush grass of the college the sprinklers made me realize I had to go to the bathroom. Now.

Ah, the rebellion of teenagers! The four of us decided to relieve ourselves outside then we began brainstorming other appropriately subversive behavior. We eventually decided to ring people's doorbells and run away, rediscovering the childhood joy of peeking from behind a parked car as confused people answered their doors and looked around for whoever had rung it. Man, we were jerks. But it was as fun as I had remembered it - sneaking onto some stranger's porch, getting up the nerve to ring the bell, sprinting to the nearest hiding spot in a group, my heart pounding in my ears. Then watching as the befuddled person open the door, came out, looked around, wrinkled their brow, and went back in. Scoping out the next house. It was almost as fun as trick-or-treating.

10:00 came all too quickly, calling us in to sleep like the good girls most adults believed we were. But our clean-cut appearance was a lie and good girls we weren't, well, not that night anyway. We acted nice briefly, saying thank you and good night to Elaine's suspicious parents. We turned on MTV and ate some chips and Boston Baked Beans and drank pop. Elaine called Freaky Mike and engaged in a mindless conversation, then she peeked upstairs. All was clear. The parents were asleep and we were free.

The walk through the star-spotted darkness was brief and giddy. The anticipation of a party! We were going to join the ranks of bona fide teenagers by drinking and making out in an unsupervised environment. Forget that none of us had actually done any of these things, we were ready to grow up already.

Scott's stinky grimy apartment glowed at the end of the block; we moved toward it like moths. I had been there before of course, since he was my brother's neighbor. But always before it had been daylight - the TV blaring, Scott hung over on his ratty couch. Tonight, though, the stereo was blaring some unrecognizable noise and the apartment was full of a bunch of Scott's skater buddies. Monica joined a scraggly-haired skater on the couch while Elaine and Berny visited with Scott and Mike in the dirty kitchen. I was relieved to see that my brother wasn't there, I may have been feeling rebellious, but I didn't want my family to find out. But I was disappointed I didn't see any cute guys worth flirting with. Most of the guys left, yelling something about a party down the block at Janelle's house as they headed out the door.

Monica tore her eyes from scraggle-head long enough to give me a look that said we can't go there and I nodded. Janelle was a few years older than us, a student at the community college and a legitimate partier who had her own cool apartment. Understandably, she hated us and all of our friends - in her eyes we were children to young to be tempting these older guys and we had no business coming to parties she was involved in. She had chased us away from a couple of killer parties earlier in the year, and none of us were eager to have a confrontation with her again. Looking back with adult eyes I chuckle and send Janelle a silent thank-you for making it impossible for me to go to parties where I did not belong. But at the time I thought she was mean. It looked like a small party at Scott's was all we were going to get this evening. Foiled again.

I decided to make the best of it. This was my chance to try drinking beer. My parents had no idea where I was and would never find out. I had friends nearby who would take care of me... and I was a teenager, definitely past due for tasting alcohol. Seeing an open beer growing like a weed from the garbage-strewn coffee table, I snatched it up and swigged it down. It tasted disgusting. Drinking as fast as possible seemed like the only way to get it down. When I looked up from my task of trying to see what drunk felt like, I saw my friends all chatting to different guys who had stayed behind, I tilted the warm beer back and finished it. Disgusting again, but mission accomplished. I leaned back on the orange couch and, always the thinker, I began to analyze my reaction. I felt light-headed and dizzy, slightly removed from my body.

One of the guys dug a pack of Camels from the debris on the table and tapped out a cigarette. He turned and offered it to one of my friends. I was surprised when she accepted. I watched as he lit it for her and as she took a deep drag, giving a short hack and puffing again. I scooted over next to her, asking for a smoke. She passed me my first smoking cigarette. I placed the slightly damp end between my lips and breathed in. I could feel the the smoke traveling down my windpipe toward my lungs. I was proud of myself for not coughing. I took another drag, even bigger this time. What a mistake! One deep inhalation and the nicotine traveled directly to my head leaving me light headed and fogging my eyes. I suddenly knew I needed to throw up. Trying to act nonchalant, I smiled while handing the cigarette back to my friend. I staggered out onto the porch. I couldn't focus on anything. Sitting down on the dirty porch, I rested my head against a cool wooden pillar. I tried to focus on a tree, but it slid over to the right - ugh. I leaned over the side of the porch and puked. And puked. It was the worst misery. The Boston Baked Beans made the puke bright red under the porch light, a sight that made me even sicker.

I don't know how long I lay there, on my stomach and probably ruining my favorite purple shorts. But when Monica finally came outside to tell me she wanted to leave I had a hard time bringing myself to a seated position. We went back inside Scott's where she got Elaine and Berny while I rinsed my mouth and washed my crusty face in his overflowing kitchen sink.

The walk home was not quite as exciting. I didn't throw-up again, but I didn't feel well. Somehow this partying business didn't seem to be nearly as fun as I had imagined it would be. When we got to Elaine's it was already starting to get light. Elaine's neighbors house (who were my neighbors too, since we lived on the same block) was already lit up, which didn't surprise me since they were an older couple and probably always got up at the crack of dawn. We tiptoed as quietly as possible into the unlocked basement and into the large guest bedroom where we quickly brushed our teeth and washed our faces before climbing into the king sized bed and falling easily asleep.

The overhead light screamed on, instantly burning my eyes. I awoke abruptly to see Elaine's mom, standing in a fury in the doorway, her hands on her hips. Elaine was on one side of me, her white blonde hair spread angelically over the pillow as she slept in peace. Monica, on the other side of me, was also awake and I imagine my face looked as scared and surprised as hers.

"Elaine, get upstairs!" she hissed, not even looking at Monica, the sleeping Berny, or me.

Elaine took her time crawling out of bed, groaning about her head. She followed her mom out of the room, leaving the door open.

We couldn't hear exactly what Joyce was saying because the house is enormous and they were far away. But we could tell from the tone of her voice that she was angry. Extremely angry. Monica and I shook Berny and tried to wake her, but she was asleep and didn't even attempt to open her eyes. We both got up, pulled on the same clothes from the night before, and packed everything else into our backpacks. We were whispering quietly to each other about what was going to happen to us and about how we could have gotten caught when Elaine slammed into the room. She looked disheveled and very angry, but her blonde good looks were basically unaffected.

"You guys have to go home. My mom has called your parents." She was so furious she didn't even bother to try to sound sympathetic. She explained that our mutual next door neighbor, had seen us walk by (and probably heard us too) and had waited until a more reasonable morning hour to call. Nice.

My stomach lurched into a worried knot. I hated the thought of my parents knowing how much trouble I'd gotten into. But then I remembered that my dad was out of town for work, so I would be able to take a shower and sleep and wash my clothes before I even had to talk to anyone about this issue. Besides, both my parents were having some marital problems with their current spouses and seemed to have stopped noticing if I was coming or going or what. So I imagined it would be pretty easy to explain my way out of whatever Elaine's mom had said.

One look at Monica, though, let me know that dealing with her parents wold be a completely different story. Unlike my parents, Monica's parents were incredibly involved and strict and worried - well, maybe they were just smart, but who knows. Whatever it was that drove them, Monica wasn't allowed to get away with anything. I didn't even want to think about how they would respond to this, especially because she would have to go home and face them still wearing the same clothes from the day before.

I gave Monica a sympathetic look as we snuck as quietly as possible through the basement door - we didn't want to face Elaine's mom's after being so sneaky. Monica was too worried to even talk, and I wished her luck as she turned the corner toward her house. At my house I was grateful for the empty driveway. As I walked up it, each uphill step more difficult than the last, the only thing I could think of was how good a hot shower and clean bed were going to feel. And man, I was never going to drink beer or smoke cigarettes again. That headache was way better than any lecture could ever be.

But what a night…

Red Apple

The Red. Walla Walla may not have been a very happening place in the 1980's, but we had the The Red Apple. This was a previous Red, not our lively and sparkling new Red Monkey where people go to dance on Saturday nights, but The Red Apple where my grandparents would go to the bar on a Saturday night and then again for brunch on Sunday morning. The Red Apple where college students could drink coffee and study next to teenagers out until curfew eating French fries and drinking chocolate malteds. The pay phone was down the hall near the bar where music and loud laughter would float out into the quieter dining area.

One of our own local historians, Joe Drazan, recently sent me information about the The Red Apple. I had fun reading an ad from the early 1970's about an entire Turkey dinner for $1.50. Is that even possible? I suppose if I were to investigate salaries and grocery prices a dollar and a half wouldn't really be that unreasonable... but it makes me wonder how much my children will be paying for a turkey dinner in 30 years!

When we were in high school The Red was one of the few places where we could hang out in the evening. We could sit in one of the blue vinyl booths eating fries, the noise from the bar wafting toward us whenever someone would open the door, drunks stumbling by on occasion, trailing smoke. This was back in the day when people could still smoke inside, though I didn't know that many kids who did. Smoke, I mean, not just smoke inside. Like me, a few kids tried it with varying degrees of bad outcomes and it just wasn't a cool thing to do.

1948

Thank goodness for places like The Red Apple, though, places to go for that those of us who maybe didn't fit in at the high school. My greatest desire was to be one of those good kids who wore a letterman jacket and went to all the games and painted my face blue and white for spirit day, but it's hard to participate when you don't make the team. And at a really big high school there just weren't enough spots. I think it is a lot better now, I believe the staff makes a much bigger effort to include all kids, but back in the early 1990's I didn't really want to be a spectator, I wanted to be a participant, so I had to go out and find other venues than my school.

Once Upon a Mattress

I eventually found a niche in the Little Theater. My mom encouraged me to audition for a play, 'Once Upon a Mattress' and I ended up with a small role. I learned quickly that, though there may be small roles, everyone on the cast is very important. Although I played a maid and was also the youngest person on the cast, I had so much fun doing this first play! I may not have fit in as well as I wanted at school, but I truly belonged at the theater. Finally, here were other people who were slightly different, who loved to sing and dance, who enjoyed costumes. I had found my place.

Remember that dance I had gone to my Freshman year? The one where I didn't really have that much fun because I was too immature? At that first dance my date Jason was a really nice guy, but I was just too shy to really do anything except, well, slouch around foolishly in my fancy dress. He was really brave to even ask me and I couldn't even muster up the courage to get out there and dance. Well later that same year, when I was in 'Once Upon a Mattress' I got to go to another dance, but this time more at my speed. I went to Spring Formal with a whole bunch of kids from the cast and we wore our costumes. I didn't really like my costume, it was brown so enough said, but being with a big crowd was so fun! We even went out and danced for a minute before getting our picture taken.

It was during my first play that I discovered something about theater: the real action takes place backstage. Sure, there is a show going on with singing and dancing and costumes and fanfare, but downstairs in the green room, where the rest of the cast is waiting, is where you really want to be. I've been in plays with big, fun casts, where people almost didn't make it onstage because we were having too much fun in the green room. In fact, just this past summer when I was in The Music Man I missed the biggest number, 76 Trombones, because one of the stage moms and I were laughing over a silly text message…in the green room. Yes, even adult stage veterans forget that backstage isn't the most important part of the show.

The wildest play I was ever in was 'Alice in Wonderland.' What a bunch of trouble makers! OK, not really, I loved those guys. It was a huge cast with a lot of very small roles so we spent a lot of time in the green room, just talking and playing cards. There was a good mixture of ages, not too many teenagers or too many grouchy adults. The people who deserved big roles had big roles. The novices had small roles. The directors knew what they were doing. It was a good situation. Not to mention people really liked to have fun, which is always a bonus.

I was single at the time and had a funny little love intrigue going on, I think everybody did. Being theater, it was mainly girls, but the few men we had gamely flirted with everyone. There was one guy in particular who I'd better not name who was very popular with the ladies. He had these beautiful green eyes and a deep bass voice and he knew just what to say to girls. I found out later he had four sisters, so this may have helped him. But this guy was trouble! He was a blatant flirt who kept attempting to get me to give him a ride home - but I didn't quite trust him and kept my distance. He would find opportunities to sit next to me and then whisper to me how beautiful I was or how good I smelled.

He had a role that put him onstage all alone for about ten minutes and one night we were all cozily sitting downstairs when one of the girls mentioned that she had given him a ride home and slept with him. Then three other girls revealed that they had too! Ha! By the time the guy came back downstairs not one girl would talk to him.

Music Man

Band Boys from the Music Man

Walla Walla also has another theater venue, the summer outdoor theater held at the Fort Walla Walla Amphitheater. The year they did The Music Man my children and I were part of the cast, Natalie was a trombone girl, Noah a band boy, and I was a Pickalittle Lady. We had so much fun getting to know the other 95 or so people working on the show as we learned songs and dances. When we weren't on stage we enjoyed the beauty of the amphitheater: the lovely outdoor surroundings, the birds, and the impromptu games of tag and hide and seek.

My children had such a great time with the other kids in the cast. My son, who loves the company of teenagers, instantly picked out a young lady, a dark-haired soprano, as his future girlfriend. He was generously supportive, though, of a more age-appropriate young man who was his rival. It was wonderful to watch my daughter sing and dance with the other little girls. Natalie is becoming very independent, so I had to admire her from a distance; but it made me happy to see her be part of something so positive. Love intrigues and new friends aside, though, the best part of all this was watching both my children get to play characters from small-town Iowa in 1920. The music and dancing were cheerful and the premise of the show is uplifting.

This is not my first experience at the Fort Walla Walla Amphitheater. In 1985 I played a townsperson in 'The Sound of Music.' My good friend Jeana and I were in the third grade and it was the highlight of my summer. Over the years many things have remained the same at the amphitheater – the rustic and beautiful surroundings, the quality and popularity of the performances, and many of the talented actors. But for me I was so happy to be able to participate with my own children. Though I have participated in community theatre since childhood, I haven't had many opportunities to do theatre since my children were born. It has been exciting to re-enter the world of performing. I feel lucky to live in a place where we can participate in events like this and even luckier that my kids are willing to join me!

Erin's 30th

I had some fun in my late 20's and early 30's. When my friend Erin turned 30 we all drove up to Seattle to celebrate with her and it was a great night. We went to a dance club where I felt, at the old age of 30, too elderly to really be able to participate. But that was just a mindset, Erin and a couple of our other friends were perfectly suited for the industrial Seattle environment, wearing silky tank tops and high-waisted shorts with spiky high heels. But even if I didn't feel cool or beautiful that night I still had fun with my girlfriends and when they turned the lights on at the end of the evening I was standing out in front of the club chatting along with everyone else. At one point I leaned up against a tree, all cool, leaning my head into the palm of my hand as I rested against the trunk. Then we got our taxi and drove home.

Rebekah and I slept together in our sleeping bags on the floor of Erin's living room. When we woke up in the morning I felt something weird in my armpit: mint gum. Someone else's gum! Almost for sure it had come from that tree I had leaned up against at the end of the night. You know it is a good night when you wake up with someone else's gum in your armpit.

Smith Rock

Somehow I eventually grew up and lost that ability to just roll with whatever was happening. I think it was about age 25 when I went to visit a friend in Portland and had to sleep on the living room floor. A few years before I would have been fine with this, no problem. Dusty floor? Dirty dishes near my head? Waking up with a dog sharing my pillow? Pshaw, I can sleep anywhere. But as I got older I realized I needed things to be a little more comfortable.

I knew I was a full-fledged grown up when I tried to join my little brother Daniel at Smith Rock one summer. Of course, I knew I was a grown up at this time, I must have been about 35 so I had no delusion of youth; but I had up until this Smith Rock excursion always considered myself to be a real go-with-the-flow type of person. Yeah. I'm really not as cool as I thought.

When I pulled up at the "camp" in my shiny Toyota 4-Runner, I joined Daniel and two of his friends. It was at least 100 degrees outside and there was not one inch of shade anywhere in the camp - not unless you count the shade the dogs were taking advantage of under their owners' vehicles. Daniel and his friend had parked their vehicles right next to each other and draped a tarp between them to create a small shelter and it was here that they were relaxing, crouching in the dirt over a small camp stove. Daniel's white pop-top Volkswagen van was open and he was busily cooking, grabbing ingredients and materials from inside the messy van. He was stirring what looked to be soup, though it was bright green so I can't say for sure. Everyone was really friendly and began telling me about their day climbing, describing in great detail the different routes and conditions they had enjoyed that day.

I'm not as into climbing as Daniel, not even half as much. Maybe not even 10% as much. I really like climbing, it is fun to get together with everyone and wear cute rock climbing outfits and talk about which route everyone wants to do. I truly love the concentration required in climbing: where to put your foot, which protrusion to grab, which direction to go. Getting to the top is such an accomplishment, and there is such a sense of freedom and success in reaching your goal, overcoming the fear of getting there. Repelling down is a thrill, too, putting your faith completely in the person at the other end of the rope, knowing you will die if things aren't tied up right. Taking that first horrifying drop backward, kicking off and out, sliding down, down, down. Finally reaching the bottom, a better person for having climbed that particular climb.

Then I'm ready for a snack and a break.

But not Daniel. There is a reason I work as a teacher and a writer and Daniel works as a professional athlete. I have interest in athletics only as a peripheral pastime, something to do briefly, something to do as entertainment, something to do to connect with other people. But Daniel sees sports as the goal itself. Since he was tiny he has had the ability to stay focused on a physical challenge for extended periods of time. Just like I can sit for hours reading or writing or researching information, Daniel can spend hours perfecting his baseball pitch or doing an ollie on the skateboard or mastering the left-footed soccer goal. As a climber he can spend hours, days, weeks trying different routes, being the first person to attempt a new approach, putting in the very first bolts so other people can climb too or seeking out new areas to climb.

It was about this time the soup was done. Daniel had been doctoring his green soup, stirring it and adding spices until he proclaimed it perfect.

He asked if anyone wanted some as he spooned some into his own sierra cup. I hate to admit it, but my cool youthful indifference to germs had long-since evaporated and I just couldn't muster any enthusiasm for the soup. I politely declined, thankful for the sandwich I had eaten shortly before arriving. One of Daniel's friends said he would like some, but he didn't have a cup. Daniel looked around for a second and spotted a silver mug sitting in the dust nearby. Picking it up he dumped out what looked like hot chocolate, gave it a little shake, then dipped the entire cup into the green soup pot before handing it to his grateful friend.

"Are you sure?" He asked me, indicating the soup.

I was pretty sure.

Later we went climbing. I really enjoyed myself, not to mention I felt really proud, after I climbed up one of the cliff walls. I was the only person around who was not extremely fit, tan, and younger than 25 and I was pretty keen not to call attention to my adultness. But after about an hour of climbing and watching all the kids climb in, still, 100 degree heat with no shade, I needed a break. Like I needed some ice water, a comfy hammock under a tree, and a good chick-lit novel. I wandered away, clutching my half-full gallon jug of water and started up the trail toward where I thought camp was. Only I must have had more sun on my never-sees-sun body than I realized because I started getting kind of dizzy and disoriented. I couldn't remember which way we had come from and I was getting more and more confused. Just as I was starting to wonder if I was going to end up in the newspaper as a victim to heatstroke, found days later wandering in the wilderness, I heard voices. I looked up the trail and was quite surprised to see three ladies walking toward me, sauntering really, chatting happily. Not one of the ladies had any water. They were all pleasantly plump and dressed like they were on their way to work, one even had on a dress. A dress! Here I was dying of heat exhaustion, lost in the wilderness and these ladies are strolling along like nothing.

They kindly helped me find my way back to camp. It turns out they were teachers too, on a tour of Smith Rock after attending a conference in nearby Bend. They reassured me that I probably had gotten a touch of heatstroke as they drove me the very short distance back to the dusty parking lot the kids called a campground. As I thanked them, waving as they drove away, I realized I was over the youthful adventure thing. I like being comfortable. Kind of like the morning I woke up staring in the friendly black face of my friend's dog and knew I could from that point forth pay for myself to stay in a hotel rather than sleep on floors. I knew at this moment that I could let young kids like Daniel camp in the dust and eat weird food between climbing a mountain all day.

By the time my brother came back to camp as the sun was setting I cooled down and I felt a lot better. But I was still ready to go home. I took him out to breakfast the next day before leaving, proud of him for being so adventurous. But I had a clean cool house and a hammock calling my name. I'm a grown up.

Daniel works packing parachutes in his spare time

Names

Names are so important, since earliest childhood I have imagined what I would name my own child. I always loved naming my stuffed animals; in fact in Kindergarten I had a whole fleet of them named Stephanie, if it was a good enough for one, it was good for everyone. And then of course there were my special dolls that had their own names: Michael Jackson, my teddy bear Jenny, the giant red mouse named, appropriately, Big Red. Even my older brother had a special stuffed animal, Clem the Dog,

I know how important a name is, when I had my own children I put a little more thought into naming them than when I was a child. Especially with a last name like Van Donge - a kid already has a mark against him with a name like that. Van Donge is just ripe for teasing, though with a name so obvious we get over it really fast, I mean who's going to get upset about getting called Ding Dong when I've heard it since Kindergarten? It's not even a clever insult, come on. Not to mention, there are so many of us we've all warned each other and laughed about it long before anyone at school could figure out that our last name is silly. In fact, my cousin Chad took the name thing one step further by having The Donger added to his golf bag. My favorite though, is when people ask me if I'm related to other Van Donges around town. I always want to say, no, Van Donge is a really common name, I have no idea who

Greg Van Donge is. Although this doesn't make me laugh as much as when people ask me if I'm related to people who are named Van Dyke. Ummm......

That's right up there with when people ask my little brother Daniel if he knows somebody who lives in another city who also has dreadlocks. Yes, all people who have dreadlocks know each other.

But back to names. I had to make sure my kids' names were pretty normal. Even though I was tempted to name my child Slingshot Mercury, somehow I knew that Slingshot Mercury Van Donge was just not going to cut it when it came to sailing through life. I think as a parent we should probably give our children the gift of getting by in the world as comfortably as possibly. You know, they should learn how to be self-sufficient, how to get along with other people, how to solve their own problems...and they probably shouldn't have a really messed up name. As a teacher I have seen hundreds, wow after 16 years, thousands of names. And names carry a lot of connotation, whether we want to admit it or not. I was fascinated when I read the chapter about names in Freakonomics by Steven D. Levitt, especially the part where he breaks down the education levels of parents based on what they name their children. My kids' names? Exactly under my education level. Cue Twilight Zone music. Especially because I didn't just pull their names out of a hat, after a lot of deliberation I decided to name them after grandparents.

I laugh sometimes and wonder what it would be like if we named our children after our parents generation. I don't know why I think it's so funny to think of toddlers named Greg or Jerry or Linda or Debbie but it makes me chuckle. But, hey, when I was a kid I used to think names like Eleanor and Hazel were funny too, and now they are pretty. In fact, names get recycled and my grandparents generation is a really common place to get great names. I guess that's how names like Sofia or Olivia, rare for girls my age, are really popular for girls my daughter's age. My name was very common, I think in my grade at school there were five or six Saras. I have a few friends named Sara. And my mom, Linda, said her name was so popular in her grade that one year there were three Lindas in her class so they had to call her Linda Lou, hee hee.

Choosing a name is tricky; something that once you choose it you can't go back on. It can take awhile to get used to calling a baby by their name, too. With both of my kids I called them The Baby for a couple of months before their name really stuck. But now I can't imagine either one of them as anything else. Natalie is feminine just like her name and Noah is peaceful yet silly, which suits his name too. Neither one has ever tried to change their name, unlike me when I was three or four and insisted on being called Baby Chicago, so I take that as a good sign. But, like my mom and me, I somehow managed to give both of them pretty common names. How does this happen? I like to think it's because we are connected to the Collective Consciousness. Yes, that's it.

Demolition Derby

The Demolition Derby is Walla Walla's biggest, most attended event. This fact, given to me by my friend Dean when he invited my family to our first 'Demo', surprised me. Even though I have heard people talk about the Demolition Derby and I had heard the roar and crash of the trucks, I had never realized what fun it was.

I loved it so much I attended a Combine Derby in Lind, Washington with my cousin Drew. Not only is there a regular demolition derby with cars and trucks, but there was an added element of entertainment when a young man asked his girlfriend to marry him in the middle of the derby. The derby in Lind is a surprisingly lively and crowed event taking place in the middle of wheat fields and hills. Lind is a tiny town and there isn't a whole lot going on between here and there. The first year Drew and his friends invited me I was a little dubious about whether or not there was actually an event. We drove and drove over yellow hills and past farms seeing almost no other vehicles. For two hours. I was open for an adventure, but I was beginning to think maybe this would be no more than a very long car trip only to end in another very long car trip. I was surprised, however, when we came around a turn on a sharp descent into a valley towards Lind. There, in the middle of all this yellow wheat and not much more, was a huge field full of cars and trucks and stands packed with people. My cousin and his friends were so amazingly prepared, they brought juice and chips and sandwiches which we enjoyed before heading inside the arena. We settled into the stands and watched cars kick up dust and mud and tear into each other. And when the combines came out we hollered along with the rest of the crowd. I even ventured into the beer garden which was jam packed with cowboys drinking Coors Light. It was so much fun!

The following year we went again and I was even more prepared – I wore a big hat and hiking boots to ward off the sun and dust, plus I brought my own juice and sandwich supplies so I could contribute to the picnic. The first year I went I wore a Carhart jacket, jeans, and cowboy boots – an unnatural clothing choice for me, since I prefer what some might call more of a hippie style. But Dean had given me the brown industrial style jacket as a gift, so when he invited me I wore the jacket, it seemed appropriate for the occasion. I was surprised when I arrived to see as many different styles of clothes as people, no need to wear the cowboy costume after all. However, do know it is possible to get pretty dusty – even extremely muddy – so be prepared!

Model T Ford races, 1939. The pre-cursor to the Demolition Derby.

Dogs

Bluedog, the best dog in the world

I had a dog and his name was Blue
I bet you five dollars he's a good dog, too

Like the song, I too had a dog named Blue. I usually dislike dog
stories because I can't stand the Old Yeller tragedy of so many of them –

and yes, my Bluedog has passed on…but I'm not going to talk about that.

Blue was The Best Dog in the World. Really. Everyone agreed. He was polite and quiet, never needed a leash, didn't beg or jump or run away, he was just a good companion. After I was divorced and on my own with my kids I was not very calm and I had a lot of trouble sleeping at night. Every small noise would wake me and once I was awake I would check all the windows and doors and listen closely to hear if anyone might be (hunting me down to kill me) outside. It wasn't until I got Blue again that I was finally able to sleep That dog was a Godsend. My ex-husband had taken him in the divorce. I hadn't wanted him to, but I wasn't strong enough to argue and I was frankly so thankful he didn't want to argue about the kids or money that I was willing to agree to almost anything else. So when, about a year after the whole situation, he sent an email asking if I could take Blue, he needed to move and couldn't, I was thrilled. I suddenly had my Mighty Protector back and the effects were immediate.

Although Blue was the furthest thing from being a vicious attack dog it was as though he were with his extra ears and nose and maturity around my house. Finally, here was someone else to patrol the house in the night and make sure no one was climbing in a window or hiding under a bed when we got home from school. From the moment he arrived back home I was able to sleep at night, I was calm, I felt secure.

We would take him to the disc golf course out at Ft. Walla Walla and he was everyone's mascot. He would stay right by our heels, unless he saw a pesky rabbit or squirrel, then he would tear off after it – though he never once caught one. When my kids and I went to the playground, Blue would play on the slides. He loved it! He would run up the structure and then zoom down the slide. Kids from all over would gather around to watch. And in the morning when I would wake, Blue would come next to my bed and say hello, letting me pet his soft black fur. I really miss that dog.

A local cattle dog working a cattle drive.
Bluedog dreamed of working as a cattle dog someday.

My dad had a dog named Jack, who was similar to Blue – he even loved playground equipment. Except Jack was delightfully rotten. He was a terrible glutton who would beg, steal food, and run away. There are so many more funny stories about Jack than Blue because Jack – though quiet, polite, and respectful – was just a ridiculous foodie. He would run away at any opportunity, always ending up at some downtown eating establishment. His two favorites were Saturday Market and Starbucks. He would take himself on a walk downtown and come back hours later with a full belly. On one of these excursions he returned with his name written with permanent marker on his collar. No one ever confessed to doing this, but it was good to know that, at least from then on, people knew his name.

Jack ended up with diabetes, no surprise considering his voracious appetite. He had to be given an insulin injection twice a day. My dad would give him a carrot at the same time, I guess to distract him from the pain – though being a dog Jack inhaled the carrot so fast I always wondered if he was aware of actually consuming it. Jack and his contemporary Snickers loved to go on walks. All we had to do was say "walk" or "out" or "leash" and they both went crazy. Even better, as we were walking, just by saying the word 'Cat' we could get both dogs straining at their leashes in a frenzy. Always entertaining.

Now my dad and stepmom Liz have two Jack Russell Terriers who mainly serve as reminder to how cool Jack and Snickers used to be. No! Sorry, I didn't write that Dad, sorry! I meant to say Quimby and Rocco are delightful and brilliant and I love being around them. Actually, Quimby and Rocco do have their charm, as small dogs tend to. They may yip and bark when you first walk in the door, but they can be really funny too. Rocco in particular is hilarious when he runs around the house squealing. This may have something to do with his condition, he has seizures and has to take daily medication for it. Barbiturates. My dad likes to say Rocco wanders around drunk most of the time. I guess this is better than Quimby who tears around barking, but that's just my opinion. I feel bad for Rocco though because he rarely barks and is pretty mellow (obviously, he's on barbiturates) but he often gets lumped together with Quimby as an annoying dog. She barks enough for two dogs, but we love her anyway.

But Quimby and Rocco are dog saints compared to my Nanny's dog, a wretched Chihuahua named Sandy. Ugh. Sandy would hide under the couch and when you sat down he would snap his little teeth out and …. bite your ankle!!! Evil little thing, I'm sorry I can't think of anything nice about Sandy, I think he may have given me a fear of sitting on couches for the rest of my life. My Aunt Janet now also has chihuahuas, but they are nothing like Sandy. Good thing, too, or I might have blamed the entire breed. In fact, I took refuge in Janet's house after leaving my ex-husband, and I wasn't really sure about her little white poof of a chihuahua named Bella. But Bella was a sweet little dog who would move from bed to bed in the night, making sure to sleep with everyone. She was a good comfort too.

I have had many lovely dogs in my life, my friend Erin's family had a Red Setter named General. Great dog. Stoic, polite, reserved. My Aunt Elva and Uncle Jerry had this sweet Black Lab named Ebony that was calm and friendly and well-behaved, just what a dog should be. Even the slightly obnoxious ones have been a positive addition to my life. In fact, now that Blue has been gone for over a year, I am now ready and on the lookout for the next-to-the-Best-Dog-in-the-World!

Dating in the Computer Age

To hear me talk one might infer that I hate all technology. I often reminisce about the days of yore when people had to speak face to face or when we weren't interrupted by texts and cell phone calls. I generally write by hand and grudgingly type it onto a computer. We do not have Wi-Fi or cable, my poor kids are stuck watching whatever DVD I have ordered for them from Netflix. But I don't really hate technology, just what can happen to relationships if we let it overwhelm us. In fact, some people are pretty surprised when I reveal to them that my Master's degree is in….Technology. Who knew? Yes, many years ago, I studied Information and Technology, a fact that directly relates to my sparing though purposeful use of computers today. Think about it.

But dating. Ugh. Dating. Not the whole going out with a cool person for a fun evening, but the initial part of dating. The job interview part. The scared I'm going to be bludgeoned or harassed or maybe dismissed or humiliated part. And the internet makes these encounters oh so easy. It is rare to hear the "Hey, I have a friend who is single….." or even more rare, "Hi, my name is_____, you seem interesting, can I have your phone number?" And who can blame people? Poor men, the nerve it must take to approach a woman and ask her out. No wonder so many people rely on the internet to find potential companionship. I took the plunge last spring and, at the urging of five different people who are happily attached thanks to the internet, started an account on an internet dating site. I put my little pictures and wrote my little bios and added all the great things about myself. I sent messages, exchanged pleasantries, and even went on 6 or 7 dates. All fine. But it is so scary. As a small town girl, a girl who has been surrounded by friends and family and recognizable faces for the majority of my life, meeting up with a complete stranger with no one to recommend him but himself is terrifying. And I don't mean terrifying as in "are these jeans cute?' but terrifying in a true crime novel kind of way.

I don't think men realize that when they text a woman they have never met four or five times a day it can be…..scary. Yes, I love a nice daily text, if you are my boyfriend. But if we have one date planned next week? Creepy. But not as intimidating as the men who think they are clever when their second or third email is a recitation of all the things they discovered about me by stalking me on the internet. Yes, I know I am a teacher and I was in a few plays and I got third place in a disc golf tournament. It is not cute when someone I do not know hunts me down and informs me that he is spying on me. What next? Did you notice when you peaked in my windows that I made lasagna last night?

I just miss the days when dating was more personal. We didn't have the internet, or we did but no one wanted to waste their time using it. We had parties and football games and radio shows to go to. Who had time to look at a blinking green cursor on a black screen? There was no Facebook or Google or Texting. We had to speak in person, or call, maybe leave a message on an answering machine. The idea of meeting someone on a computer was comical. Looking for potential love required people to go out into the world, ask for help, take great risks. And stalking was a literal thing, not a general concept related to search engines and social media.

Yes, the internet can be a really good way to meet people. I recently asked an older couple how they had met. The man was so cute, he grabbed his wife's hand and said, "The old-fashioned way, the internet." Awwww. But for me, I will just rely on the great intervention of God or friends or luck or whatever used to let people meet and fall in love. I'll leave the complications of internet dating to more valiant people.

Wi-Fi

Does this mean I may have some issues with trust and relationships today? Ha ha, it might. After six years I have finally allowed someone into my life well enough that my kids know him and I don't do strange things like break up with him every couple of weeks or panic if he doesn't call me for a day or two. In fact, I'm really content with this guy.

But I'm also fragile and suspicious and very hesitant. Recently, he helped me get set up with a computer and internet at my house. I hadn't had a computer since three years previously when three year old Noah had accidentally dive bombed onto the bed where my laptop sat open, destroying it. This was the laptop I had bought to replace the laptop I had spilled a full bottle of water all over as I tried to pass it to five year old Natalie. Sigh.

So, this special man, Paul, was helping me to get everything I needed so I can finally stop writing by hand and with my thumbs onto my cell phone and actually work on compiling my million pages of work into one or two published books. He loaned me his ridiculously expensive Mac, which I treat like a newborn baby and will not let my children even look at, and then he arranged for internet service. I was so thankful.

118

However, when I first logged on to my first ever Wi-Fi, it was not called something cool like all the Wi-Fi signals I see all over town (Aussie, Jen'sNet!, Ourhouse),I was ready for my internet to be named something sparkly and feminine, but in fact he had set it up without even asking me what I wanted my Wi-Fi to be named. And, worse, he had named it Paul. Paul! And more suspicious, the password was somebody else's phone number. I was confused, and when I asked he didn't have any explanation, just a shrug and a vague promise in his quiet way to try to change it someday.

Every time I logged on to my Wi-Fi I was reminded of the fact that once again it looked like maybe I might be with someone who didn't respect me. I quietly thought about it for a couple of days, then I decided to just call the internet provider and change the name of my WiFi to my own name. In the meantime I had spent the past two days kind of ignoring him, not sure if he was actually as wonderful as I had thought. Did he think he had some type of right to my internet, just because he had spoken to the person to set it up? I mean, yes, this was kind of him, but I'm the one paying the bill. Would he be like this with other things, just inserting himself without even asking my opinion? By the time the kindly East Indian man named John from the internet company got to my call I was kind of worked up. Maybe no one would ever treat me well! Maybe I had some innate magnet in me that attracted men that would abuse me. After talking to John for a few minutes I finally understood that the reason my internet was called Paul was not because Paul had arbitrarily named it after himself but because his router came from his house in Portland and the router had the name already, the password was his old password. I blubbered on about it to John, about how I'd been worried that maybe Paul hadn't been quite who I thought and how relieved I was that it wasn't this at all. John laughed and said in his polite clipped English that he was happy to help me. Yeah, happy to help me with my psychological problems!

New Year's Eve, 1995

THERE IS ROOM FOR ANOTHER ONE
IN WALLA-WALLA, WASH.

HOW ABOUT YOU?

I'm glad I met Paul.   Actually I don't even remember meeting him because I always just knew him. We went to school together from junior high on, though I didn't know him well as he was two years ahead of me in school. But when I was in high school and became friends with Kim I started seeing Paul around. He was her brother Scott's best friend and all of us would go to the same social events. Paul was quiet and polite and we would often talk, though I don't remember specifically about what.

It wasn't until after high school that I have any real memory of him. I was dating Jeremy, a nice young man who came to visit me when I went to college in Guadalajara, and I was in Walla Walla for New Year's Eve. Jeremy and Christine and I went to a party near the Whitman Campus and it was packed with people. I was 19 and it was the first time I had ever been to a New Year's Eve party. There was loud music and people were dancing and talking and having a great time. Once the New Year's countdown started everyone blew party horns and screamed and yelled and started hugging. Jeremy came up and gave me a chaste kiss and moved on, then Paul was by my side. He grabbed my hand and pulled me toward him and gave me my first real kiss. I was moved to my toes and never forgot that kiss, not even 18 years later when Kim mentioned Paul to me.

"Do you remember Scott's friend Paul?" Kim asked as our kids splashed in her swimming pool.

I laughed and relayed the New Year's kiss story, how I'd never really seen Paul again after that but how I'd never forgotten him.

Then we moved on to telling our kids not to dunk each other.

About a month later Kim invited me to her older brother Scott's 40th birthday party. My kids were visiting their dad for the evening and I was happy to have a social event to distract me so I readily agreed. I pulled a dress over my swimsuit and rode my bike across town to Kim and Scott's parent's house. As soon as I walked out to the pool I spotted Paul and I knew I'd been set up and I was so glad! He totally ignored me after saying a brief hi, but I wasn't going to let him off the hook. After he went in the house and hid out to watch the Mariners I went in and got him, inviting him to come out and chat. He insists he would have come out to talk to me eventually…but I never really gave him a chance. I remembered that New Years kiss.

He ended up driving me home late that night after we had talked and talked and talked by the pool, he dropped me off and asked for my phone number, calling me a few days later to invite me to go huckleberry picking. And from there I finally found someone I could trust and enjoy and I'm so thankful.

I ❤ ❤ Walla Walla

I know kids are supposed to be embarrassed by their parents sometimes, otherwise we would probably stay home as a financial burden for the rest of our lives. But my dad seemed to go to a little more effort than my mom to be embarrassing. Besides his green VW van with Nuke the Whales on the bumper he would also on occasion walk around wearing his bicycle helmet. The fact that I myself now do this might be a testimony to how overly sensitive I was as a kid. Possibly most embarrassing, though, was that he also liked to wear a bright yellow t-shirt that had I ❤ ❤ Walla Walla stamped across the chest, he won it on a radio contest through Whitman College's radio station, KWCW. He wore this shirt proudly, puffing out his chest if I, in my young teen narcissism, complained about it being embarrassing.

My mom embarrassed me less as a kid. Mind you, I didn't walk around thinking she was cool or anything weird, either, I was as bratty as the next kid. But she didn't draw attention to herself like my dad did. Sometimes now as an adult she can be a little - ah, exuberant - and if it weren't so funny, I might cringe a little. Like when we are at the movie and she speaks at a regular volume. But I know I lucked out with my mom. I think she is making up for her mom, my Nanny, who may have been a bit of a handful as a mother. Cheerful and chatty and just a wee bit wild, my Nanny tends to stand out in a crowd. For a granddaughter it is funny, for my mom, though, I think it may have been a little embarrassing. Take smoking, for example. Nanny started smoking a corn cob pipe at the age of 6. You read that right, 6. It was Oklahoma. It was three quarters of a century ago. Smoking was good for you back then! (OK, it wasn't). Nanny likes to light up while still indoors, taking a little puff as she walks outside. She thinks no one will notice - believe me, we notice. Nanny also likes to borrow her neighbors' flowers, and their flower pots. And sometimes their yard decorations. Somehow people notice this too.

My own kids, on the other hand are stuck with me as a mom. They aren't generally too annoyed with me when I dress weird, sing in public, dance funny, or clean their faces with spit. But they will grow older and learn to be embarrassed of me...I hope!

Live Bands

I love our downtown, especially on Friday and Saturday nights when we have so much live music and entertainment. It wasn't always this way, even ten years ago the most we could hope for would be the yearly street dance or the occasional live band. And of course Barnabys....which I am the perfect age to have LOVED so don't tease me.

My mom and aunts speak fondly of dancing to live bands (and occasionally getting kicked out for being too loud) at different places:

Uncle Bobs, the 19th Hole, private parties and school dances. The idea of a live band, not a DJ or Stereo, is what made the night so much fun. At my family's suggestion I hired a band to play at my wedding many years ago and it was such an amazing experience. The marriage may not have lasted forever, but everyone still has great things to say about how much fun the occasion was and the live band had a lot to do with it.

Now live music is once again prevalent in Walla Walla. Is this a nation-wide phenomenon or is it limited to our little gem of a town? Sapolil has live music every Friday and Saturday night and if you are really lucky Bill, the owner, might even invite you to dance on the piano! Charles Smith Winery, Marcy's, Power House, and Main Street Studios also have excellent music.

OK, I've never actually seen a band this cool.
Maybe someday, though.

I enjoy taking my kids to listen to live music; Saturday Market always has talented musicians performing, and the Wheelin' Walla Walla Weekend Car Show always sponsors a street dance on Saturday following the show. Last year we had such a good time dancing to Gary Winston and the Real Deal, I look forward to hearing who they line for this September. Walla Walla is such a great place to live, I am so thankful for our lovely downtown and all the events we can go to.

Halloween

Fall is in the air and in my house we are eagerly anticipating Halloween. Now, this isn't to say we don't talk about Halloween all year. Choosing the right costume is so important the kids plan what they are going to wear beginning as early as November. Yes, one year before the holiday we start declaring what we will be. So far this past year we have planned on being the Scooby Doo gang, the Grease characters, Zombies, Easter Bunnies, and Pirates. It's a good thing my mom has made many costumes, because trying them on and planning is a big part of the fun. My only rule for costumes is that I won't go to a Halloween store and buy one. My poor kids, the costume has to be homemade.

Last year we each had three costumes. One for school (somehow dressing as a devil and a zombie at a Catholic school seemed.....wrong), one for a party, and one for trick or treating. I read once that people used to dress up so evil spirits who come out on Halloween won't recognize them, so I guess this way we're pretty safe. I had a lot of fun dressing up as Titania, Queen of the Fairies last year for an adult party. I may or may not have spent too much time talking to a Nick Bottoms-type character, but oh well, this is one of the perils of Halloween. At least I looked good.

When I was young, my friends and I used to go trick-or-treating. My aunts, Janet and Debbie, took all of us cousins few times. They would drive us around to nearby neighborhoods, drop us off at the end of one street and pick us up at one block later. I remember them telling us if we weren't good they would take us to the pumpkin patch and drop us off there and my big brother, Christian, saying he wouldn't mind. It seems at some point they actually did drive Chris to a pumpkin patch so he could show us all how brave he was.

My dad said he used to go trick-or-treating, too. I was surprised; somehow I thought this was some new event created by marketing campaigns. But no, waaaaaaay back in the 1950's (Kidding! Kidding!) people used to also dress up and go door to door seeking candy. The only difference was that back then parents weren't generally quite so paranoid as we are now. My dad said his parents, after making them go around to the neighbors' houses (half a mile away in the country) would drive them into town so they could trick-or-treat around their grandparents house. Only in those times the adults didn't wait patiently at each street corner, they just waved good-bye and knew their kids would most likely eventually come back.

Kids in a Halloween Parade in Walla Walla, 1953

The last time I went trick-or-treating I was 14. I dressed as a snowboarder, not too far-fetched a costume, considering it snowed that year! A couple of my friends and I knew it was our last shot at childhood, so we tried really hard to make ourselves look as young as possible. Not really easy, considering at 14 we were all fully-grown. But who can blame us, trick-or-treating is so much fun. Now I bring my own children trick-or-treating. I remember as a young adult when people first started taking their kids downtown in the daylight. I couldn't believe it! What an adulteration of Halloween. Trick-or-treating in daylight? At businesses? Lame. But, you know, it's fun. I love seeing all the different costumes, seeing friends and acquaintances with their kids. I don't usually let my kids wait in the long lines for the candy, I tell them they can get candy at home so not to worry – especially because we never really get any trick-or-treaters. I buy candy just in case, though, I just make sure it is something I won't eat if I'm left with a bag of it. No way are any Reeses Peanut Butter Cups or Kit Kats going to enter my home, somehow if they do I feel this obligation to eat them all. I buy Jolly Ranchers or other sour candy so there is no temptation!

Happy Halloween, don't forget your costumes. You wouldn't want those evil spirits to recognize you!

Even adult ladies love costumes: Jeri, Marika, Sara and Sarah are fierce!

Bowling

My son loves bowling. Bowling. I don't understand this obsession, I can barely break a score of 90 with bumpers, but my boy frequently begs to go bowling.

He may take after his great-grandparents, Nanny, Fafa, and Gramps all enjoyed bowling. I think this may be a societal change, it seems to me people used to bowl more. Am I wrong? I know people still bowl, especially young people at Cosmic Bowling on Saturday nights, but it seems like my grandparents generation was more likely to bowl on a league. My Mom likes to say people used to do a LOT more than they do now: clubs, lodge, baseball, PTA. Is this true? I'm not a sociologist but I wonder if TV, the internet, and almost all women having to work might have something to do with this. Oh, not to mention that being a single parent seems to be pretty common. Or maybe we all just like to idealize the 1950's because 'Leave it to Beaver' and 'I Love Lucy' are etched into our collective consciousness.

When I was young, I would go with my Mom, Nanny, and Fafa to their bowling league on Sunday afternoons. My Nanny, would give each of us kids some money. My brother and cousins would immediately spend every cent on candy, pop, and video games. Being the thrifty girl I am, I would not spend any of my money. I would watch my cousins play video games and try not to look at their treats so I wouldn't be tempted. Then I would scurry home and hide my cash in a book. Later, I started keeping score for the league players. This was, obviously, before the invention of the electronic score boards, and I loved adding the spares and strikes in my head, trying to estimate who the highest scorer would be. I also very much loved the tips Nanny and Fafa and their friends would give me. I always came home with a nice bundle of cash. Ah, those were the days!

Now I get to take my own kids bowling. Recently I took Noah while his sister was at a birthday party. We had the bumpers up and both did pretty well, I thought. It was a lot of fun spying through the floor to see the ball run up and Noah absolutely loved the cartoon images that play on the score screen after each shot. The Bowlaway has recently undergone quite a transformation with new flooring, furniture, a bar, and a video game room. In fact, we had so much fun that I agreed to bring him back the next day for a special kid's day when kids got to bowl for free.

This time I didn't make him leave after 3 games, I let him play as long as he wanted. I was surprised when he was still enthusiastically heaving the six-pound ball toward the pins after two hours. I didn't let him use the bumpers this second time so he could get an idea how to really play. At first he wasn't happy about this, but after awhile he got the hang of keeping the ball out of the gutter. Though he only scored a high of 60, he really enjoyed himself. He ended up playing 7 games. He was pretty impressed with himself when I told him he had thrown the ball 140 times!

Gramps loved bowling too. Is this some kind of genetic trait? Maybe. My cousin Chad has Gramps' ball, the finger holes fit him perfectly. I never really thought of us as a family of bowlers, but hey – who knows, maybe my boy will end up being the next King Pin!

Triumphant!

TV

Recently at lunch my colleagues and I turned to the subject of our favorite old TV shows. We all reminisced quite happily about the Cosby Show, Leave it to Beaver, and Three's Company. We decided our favorite blonde was Chrissy, we felt sorry for Janet, and Jack Tripper was a ridiculous over-actor. We all absolutely loved The Cosby Show, mainly because Bill Cosby is hilarious. I remember looking forward to it every Thursday night. And Leave it to Beaver pretty much still makes us feel inadequate as mothers. Our conversation began because of FaceTime and how much our lives are becoming like The Jetson's. Someone mentioned how she hates getting Face Time calls early in the morning when she hasn't gotten dressed yet and it reminded me of the episode where Jane Jetson puts on a "Morning Mask" to receive a Television Phone call, but then her friend's face falls off. Things have sure changed! Just like Jane Jetson, we don't always want to fix our hair just in case we get a phone call.

My children asked me to order The Brady Bunch from Netflix. With a sigh, I begrudgingly did. I have to admit it was interesting to watch this blast from the past from the very first episode, as a child I always wondered how the show had started out. Did you know the first episode had Carol (whose last name was Martin) and Mike getting married? It was sort of cute, I guess, if you can suspend belief long enough to accept that the kids immediately began calling their step-parents Mom and Dad. And more maddening (from the perspective of a mom who works full time and has no husband) is the fact that Mrs. Brady has no job PLUS a live-in housekeeper. Ugh. I was able to privately console my jealousy with the Enquirer-garnered knowledge that Florence Henderson's REAL boyfriend was Greg. Tee hee.

I enjoyed hearing the perspective of my parents and godmother. Two common themes were that kids had no say over what was on TV, this was entirely up to parents. Meaning the kids were watching things like Bonanza, The Twilight Zone, and Ozzie and Harriet. I remember that too, my grandparents made me watch Lawrence Welk and Hee Haw. Ugh. The other theme was the prevalence of variety shows like Red Skelton, The Carol Burnett Show, The Loretta Young Show, and The Smothers Brothers Show. I found it interesting that all three mentioned seeing The Beatles for the first time on Ed Sullivan, as Connie said, if you ask anyone over 60 they will remember two things: where they were when Kennedy was shot and seeing the Beatles on Ed Sullivan

And TV influenced people's lives then as now: my mom named my youngest brother Mason after one of her all-time favorite shows, Perry Mason. And my dad has this to say about advertising: "Back then cigarettes were still advertised on TV and we kids all knew the jingles. By the time we were teenagers we ALL smoked, (coincidence?), and the ads were still on TV. It was funny to take notice that whenever a cigarette ad was aired, within 10 minutes, and with absolutely no one having said a word, anybody who smoked, sitting there in the room, was smoking a cigarette. It was as if, 'Oh yeah! I'm glad that cigarette ad just played, I almost forgot to smoke!"

Now I end up watching a lot of children's movies. Unlike my grandparents, I don't dictate what is on the TV, somehow I don't think my kids should be watching Orange is the New Black or The Big Lebowski. But after being exposed to the treasure that is The Brady Bunch my daughter has discovered a whole world of vintage TV to enjoy. Our next Netflix selection? The Adams Family….we'll see what she thinks of Cousin It.

Look kids, a TV! I'm sure it won't really change our lives too much…

Blue Takes a Bath

Bathing can be kind of a struggle at our house. I'm not sure why, I think it's just the annoyance of taking time away from the fun of the day, but neither of my kids ever voluntarily bathes. Funny, though, because once I get either of them in the tub - especially Noah - then I have to force him to put the bath toys away and get out.

But getting my kids to bathe is easy compared to what it was like to get my dog Blue to bathe. He didn't just dislike bathing, he disliked water. I bet he never touched even one foot to water more than three or four times in his entire life. But his one brush with near submersion was enough to scar a few of us to the point where we never tried bathing him again.

We used to take Blue to Fort Walla Walla to run around while we played disc golf. He was so well-behaved and polite he could be off his leash and no one worried about him. One afternoon, though, he emerged from the woods smelling very ripe. Kind of a mixture of duck poop and dead animal. He wore a smug expression, especially when anyone he approached hollered and covered his nose. The scent was horrific.

My cousin Chad's sensibilities were especially offended. Chad decided Blue not only needed a bath, he needed a bath right there in Garrison Creek. Chad's plan was to invite Blue over one of the foot bridges but then quickly push him into the water so he would get washed off. Somehow it didn't quite work out that way. Chad stood in the middle of the bridge and called to Blue, who, always compliant, obeyed. But when Chad abruptly shoved him the couple of feet below into the creek, Blue would have none of it. After landing briefly in the water, he sprang onto the bank and shook off, leaving nearby Chad soaked with duck-poop-scented river water. Blue then pranced off triumphantly, now not only smelling of rotten duck poop on his back but all over his body. The smell took a couple weeks to fade away. Blue eventually smelled better too.

Soccer

The Zebralicious Girls in their matching zebra socks

My children are signed up for Fall soccer and we can't wait! Soccer is fun for the kids, yes, but I could argue that it might just be more fun for the spectators - especially the really little guys, you know, the ones who don't know how to play. Last Fall was their first experience with an official soccer team. Although their dad, Bill, is an excellent soccer player, I decided to wait until they wanted to play before I committed them to a team for a season. Natalie was with a group of her classmates and, since there were eight of them and they were all turning eight years old that year, their name was The Crazy Eights. Natalie's games were exciting and resemble real matches with people passing, goalies generally blocking goal attempts, and actual dribbling down the field. The fact that her outfit needed to be color-coordinated with her hair-tie and socks was secondary.

Noah's team, on the other hand, was comedy. Just pure comedy. First, their name - which they selected themselves: The T-Rex's. And because T-Rex is such a common soccer team name, their was another T-Rex team in his 5 and under league. So when the two T-Rex teams played each other we had to differentiate by adding their jersey colors. Go Blue T-Rex's! Go Red T-Rex's! Or more often, "No Blue T-Rex's, your goal is the other way!!!" Or, "No Blue T-Rex's, come out of the stream, leave the rocks, there is a game going on!" Yes, this is how sporting events should be. Spectators doubled over in fits of laughter as the players steal balls from their teammates, wander off the field, and where the entire game can stop when someone points out a cool cloud. And lest this get too competitive, there is no goalie - yet, somehow, the ball almost never made its way into the goal. By the end of the season (unfortunately for me) the players had learned many skills and were actually getting the hang of the sport. Sigh. I guess this upcoming season will probably be more about soccer and not watching little kids be hilarious.

Like I said, my kids' dad is a really good soccer player. Years ago, before we had children, he and my cousin Chad invited - or maybe that was insisted - Chad's wife, Stephanie, and me to join them on their city soccer league team. There is a rule with the Jack and Jill league that there be a certain number of girls on the team and also on the field, not to mention that each time the ball is in play a female has to actually make contact with the ball. Because neither Stephanie nor I is particularly good at soccer (sorry Steph - you are better than me though!) the play generally consisted of someone kicking the ball to whichever one of us was on the field and then we would quickly return it so the real play could begin. Somehow, despite my dubious contribution, our team ended up winning the city tournament that year. Like my daughter, I was generally only concerned with the color of my tee-shirt compared to my socks.

This was not my first soccer-playing experience. When I was in the second grade my older brother Christian talked me into playing on the Green Park soccer team. Back in the early 1980's soccer was not the popular sport it is today, so there were not enough interested girls to form their own team. So I was on a team with only one other girl, Ashley, with the rest of the team composed of boys. I was not the type of girl who was OK with this type of situation, boys being.....boys and all. So I never really got used to making any real effort. In fact, I doubt if I ever even made contact with the ball. I was more of the cloud-gazing, outfit matching, field abandoning type of soccer player. But despite this, I did develop an appreciation for the spirit of the sport, especially the camaraderie afterward when we got to eat the treats brought by different team moms.

I'm happy my own children have the opportunity to play now, the Walla Walla Parks and Rec soccer program is huge and each Saturday feels like a holiday because of all the people and excitement out at the Sports Complex. I love going to their games. This is not because of any particular opinion about the sport; I actually don't really understand the rules of soccer other than Run to the Goal! Kick the ball in the Goal! Guard the Goal! But nonetheless I really enjoy soccer games. All sporting events in fact. I love watching people, talking to other spectators, being outside, knowing my kids are having good, healthy fun. Oh, and the game. Yes, the game is pretty entertaining too.

When my kids started their second year playing soccer I was rewarded with new and exciting entertainment. Sure, watching Daniel, Jenna, Cole, Emerson and other really talented players is kinda fun....but I enjoy the ridiculous even more: The younger siblings running out onto the field during play, the players who exuberantly make goals for the other team or steal the ball from teammates, the kids on the bench who accidentally kick the ball back in when it is out of bounds – this is what makes kids' soccer so fun. And this year, it is the team names that are really entertaining.

My son practiced his lobbying skills by showing up at the second practice and convincing each team mate individually that the name "Green Lightning Bolts" should be their team name. His powers of persuasion were rewarded when their coach, Tim, asked what their name should be and .... Lo! They all shouted together, "Green Lightning Bolts!"

My daughter's team is Zebralicious and their coach, Jeff surprised us with matching zebra socks and headbands. Now THIS is what makes team sports worthwhile, cute uniforms! I look forward to seeing the kids play the Blue Tornados, The Super Sheep, The Black Panthers (hee hee!), The Purple Dragons, the Silver Stars, or any of the Ninja or T-Rex teams. I remember fondly my little brother, Daniel's, team names from when he played select city soccer: the Firebolts and the next year the Thrashers. Incidentally, the year they were Thrashers they made it to a large tournament. The organizers designed a T-Shirt for all the participating teams, but had inadvertently mis-printed The Thrashers as The Thrushes. Apparently the boys didn't appreciate being compared to sweet little birds; not one purchased a shirt.

As spectators, we have fun cheering for our kids, the coaches wear shirts which all wisely advise, 'They play. I coach. You cheer.' I probably don't want to know why this admonishment was necessary, but it is a great way to enjoy the game. Maybe some parents are more invested in their kids' soccer playing abilities than I am. Parents who actually know how to play soccer. I'll stick to not really understanding and cheering for any movement.

We particularly enjoyed playing at a recent game when we realized our team was playing the "Yellow Thunder." Throughout the game we had a lot of fun hollering, "Go Lightning! Go Thunder!" It was hard to hear us over the game next to us where the parents were yelling, "Go Green Ninjas! Go Blue Ninjas!" I'm not really sure who won. They weren't either. With no goalie, the score gets really high. After eight or so goals for each side, what does it matter? We were all having a good time.

Tough Mudder

Jerry, Greg, and Sara after the Tough Mudder

My family and I decided to participate in an event called the Tough Mudder. My cousin Abbie was the instigator. Now Abbie is an athlete, a life long, multi-sport amazing athlete who wins rock climbing competitions, boxing matches, and works out every single day. She recruited a team of fellow athletes to join her on a trip to Seattle for the 11-mile, 14-obstacle event designed by the Marines. Though I didn't exactly jump at the chance, I agreed my dad and my Uncle Jerry said they were doing it. I figured it would be a good motivator to get into really great shape.

I've been very physically fit quite a few times in my life. Really high strung, anxious people like me are often also in good shape. Why? For one, just being when you are always on tenterhooks and worried that the world might fall apart requires a lot of tension and energy and worry. As I sit here typing I am shaking not just one knee but both knees and wiggling back and forth. I will probably get out of my seat 3 or 4 times in the next hour, just to check on things around the room, you know, make sure the temperature is ok, the curtain is just right, the door is shut properly. I'm what you might call a sensitive person. I do not see this as a good trait, though no one else has ever pointed out the flaw. It is a most definite flaw, though. Being sensitive means I stay up all night long if one of my students complains about a book I read in class. Being sensitive means I cry for a week when my daughter starts kindergarten. Being sensitive means when I see people fighting on a movie my heart starts to race and for the next couple of hours I feel a nervous apprehension that I myself may not be safe. It makes me really annoying, especially to myself.

It can make me a good friend, though. If you have a problem or feel bad and call me, I will cry with you. If your day is going really well and you want to go out and dance and have fun I can probably muster up the good vibe too. And being naturally high-strung makes me look like I'm in pretty good shape, too, even when I forget to go to the gym for six or eight months.

Before I had children I was consistent as the sun with going to the Y for spinning workouts every Monday, Wednesday, and Friday morning at 5 am. I led exercise classes at my elementary school, too. Plus I rode my bike everywhere, walked a lot, did exercise videos. I was fit. But note, I said before I had children. After I had children I did not make time to exercise as much. Was this because I was tired? Or just comfortable at home with my kids? Or would this have happened as I neared thirty anyway? Who knows, but I stopped being maniacally fit. I got skinny because I got even more nervous, and you can hate me for that if you want. I guess skinny women deserve to be hated because so many women desperately want to be skinny. I get it. But I am no longer gaunt and I know that at that time the reason I was so skinny was because life was not good and I was extremely nervous. Some people are just skinny, just like some people are more round.

But I very much digress from the topic of the Tough Mudder. So I may have been thin, but I certainly wasn't strong, and I wanted a goal so I could get in shape. We had six months to train for this event and I drew up a plan: running daily, weight lifting, aerobic videos, yoga...I was going to be in the best shape of my life! I was going to be awesome like my little cousin Abbie!

But I didn't do it. I continued to do my very minor morning and evening yoga routine (we are talking 5 minutes each, some small stretches, nothing more) and the occasional walk. I would sometimes get nervous and pop in a Tae Bo workout video and listen to Billy Blanks tell me how great I am and feel like I was on my way to strong arms and that powerful feeling of buffdom I have felt in the past when I can get it together to get really fit. Then I would just not do anything. I don't have an explanation, it was almost like having an event like Tough Mudder looming ahead of me made me even worse than usual for exercise, it made me frozen. Like having a huge, daunting event just solidified how old and out of shape I felt. So I did nothing.

And the event arrived anyway. We all piled into two vehicles and drove 5 hours over the Cascades to Seattle. We met up with my little brother Daniel, his girlfriend Kristin, my Aunt Elva, and my Uncle Jerry. We had a big Thai dinner and drank beer and had a ton of fun catching up and talking and joking about how out of shape we were. Then the next morning we met up with my cousins and the rest of the team. The team we began to call The A Team. We discovered within the first half mile that Abbie, Josh, and three of their friends were in a different league from us, in fact these guys were in league with the marines who designed the event. Sure, we all started out together, cheerfully boosting each other over the first six foot wall and jogging the quarter mile to a barb-wire covered mud pit. We sloshed on our stomachs through the sun, proud to be covered with mud and happy for the amazingly beautiful September day. Then we reached the ice tubs.

These were 8-foot deep pools full of ice surrounded by screaming marines. We had no time to think before we were jumping in, then dunking our heads under to swim below a 3-foot wide plank. My lungs involuntarily constricted from the cold just as someone in front of me accidentally kicked me in the face, I desperately pulled myself forward and clawed my way out of that hell-pool. I was freezing wet, had a fat lip, there was no way to dry off and we still had 10 miles to go. No one else looked too happy either. We kept our jolly faces on though and started our jog up the hill toward the next obstacle when, thankfully, my dad's heart rate monitor set off a beep of alarm. He told us to go ahead, he needed to walk to avoid any heart problems. The A Team worriedly jogged in place, saying they didn't mind waiting, while Jerry and I slowed right down and valiantly volunteered to walk with him. My cousins and their friends left us behind, promising to wait at the end, while we waved them on in relief.

Abbie, Chris, Sunday, and Josh: The A Team

And from there the Tough Mudder was a pleasant experience, a relaxing stroll in the early fall sun with my dad and uncle with the occasional obstacle to liven things up. We joked and talked and told stories. We climbed ropes and trudged through mud. There were a few obstacles that stand out in my brain as challenging but still fun: carrying large logs, jumping off a high platform into a deep pool, swinging across giant monkey bars. There were a couple I couldn't do: heaving myself over a six foot wall and swinging from ring to ring over water (I fell in). And there was one I wish I had never done: the electric cords dangling down from metal wires over a muddy tarp. I died here. I say this and people kind of nod, like oh, that must have sucked. But I left my body, I was floating in clouds, they had to drag me out. I wouldn't do that again. I was crawling on my stomach through the mud with barbed wire a few inches above my back. Dangling from the barbed wire were strands of electric wire that would pulse on and off, like and electric fence. I wasn't really thinking about the effects this would have on someone with a heart-murmur when I saw that obstacle, I just saw that everyone else was going through it so I thought I would be successful too. My dad stepped around, his doctor had explicitly told him to avoid anything like this, but I was 35, I didn't give it much thought. So I started belly-crawling through. But every time the wires sent a shock through me, my body would tense up and I couldn't move, so pretty soon I was just frozen under the wire, my jaw clenched and everything turning black. The pain was so unbearable that I started dreaming or something because I was suddenly in the sky, flying over the city, looking at clouds and buildings. Then I was looking at dirt and feet as people dragged me out. They heaved me up by the armpits and I shook myself into awareness. I stumbled forward a few steps and looked at the ground, and there, coiled in the grass, was a little black snake. I stood there staring at the snake for awhile until my dad and Jerry raced over asking if I was OK. I could only mumble about the buildings and the snake for a few minutes, but I snapped out of it.

We were not last, not the absolute last, because there is a group that always brings up the rear of all the Tough Mudder competitions. They carry an American Flag and an enormous log to represent the fallen warrior. They walk slowly and deliberately and the symbolism is beautiful. So those guys stayed behind us, making us second last. We were nearly last in the 14-mile Bridge Pedal that same year. And we were last in the Balloon Stampede 5K Fun Run. And the Grand Fondo 40-mile bike ride. I guess if you can't be first last is an OK option too. At least it's something. At least we did it.

I have to include this non-sequitur of a photograph. Two original Tough Mudders: The Fabulous Moolah defeated Helen Hild at Borleske Stadium in Walla Walla in 1957.

Baseball

Since earliest childhood I have absolutely loved attending baseball games. No, not really to watch, though on occasion I might glance up at the proceedings, but for all the other fun that goes on. As a child I accompanied my parents to my older brother, Christian's, baseball games at the field behind Kmart. Chris played for Mr. Ed's and my family and I spent a lot of time out there cheering him on. I, of course, did not spend much time in the stands, preferring instead to play in the fields nearby with the other younger siblings. We would find garter snakes and wild flowers, play tag and hide-n-seek, and explore the creek nearby. At the end of the game my patience was always rewarded with an Icee Pop from the concession stand.

Later, my younger brother Daniel played baseball at the same field. He was on the PowerAde team and by this point I understood and enjoyed the game. I loved chatting with the relatives of the all the players, watching the little kids come and go from the stands as they took breaks from playing, and enjoying the triumph when Daniel's team scored a run.

Now my kids and I love going to Borleske Stadium for the Sweets Games. We love the cheering crowds, Sweet Lou, the food, and the entertainment during the game. We enjoy sitting along the third base line where we can be part of the action; my kids like to run after stray balls, bringing any to Sweet Lou for a signature. Two years ago we brought my son to watch the Sweets on his fourth birthday. Not only did he manage to snag a stray ball and get a signature, but my daughter was invited to race Sweet Lou around the field. She generously gave the honor to her little brother, so he got to go in front of the whole crowd and run the bases. He was so excited, it was a great birthday.

On occasion I will go to a Sweets game with friends instead of my children. When I do, the Beer Garden is also a fun place to watch the game, especially with the lively conversation and very close proximity to left field and the occasional foul ball. It took me a couple of years to realize there is also a Beer Garden on the other side of the field, right at the entrance. This is not as exciting or crowded as the far location, but is a good place to get a drink before heading to the stands. The hometown support continues even here with beer offerings from Laht Neppur, Blue Mountain Cider Company, and wine from Bergevin Lane, Va Piano, and Basel Cellars.

And no baseball game is complete without food. I have always enjoyed the local offerings from Andrae's Kitchen and Walla Walla Sweet Onion Sausage, though my kids are partial to the culinary delights from the concession stand. It is our routine to get a red rope, popcorn, and a pop – food I don't care for but will likely stand out in their memories like the Icee Pops from my brothers games still do for me.

Watching the Sweets isn't really so much about how amazing the venue is or even how well the team is doing. It's about how the entire experience, the people you know, getting Sweet Lou to sign a foul ball, and knowing this is our team.

Changing Vernacular

Ready to be in on the latest vernacular being used by young people in Walla Walla?

I'm relieved that I am hearing my students say one of the latest popular phrase less now than at the beginning of the school year, I'll get to this little gem in a moment; but this has me thinking about language and how it changes through the years. As a middle school teacher I have the privilege of hearing new phrases and language daily. I generally can guess at the meaning, though I admit (but never to my students!) that some of what they say is mystifying.

A dictionary of some popular phrases being used by the middle-school set in Walla Walla:

Newb: Or is it Noob? This is said only by boys to other boys in response to saying something foolish, as in, "You're such a NEWB!" I'm going to guess this comes from Newbie since no one ever gets upset.

Baller: OK, I will admit that my generation used this word in a far more adult way than the sweet innocent children of today. The first time a boy shouted this out to another boy within my earshot I put on my teacher scowl face, ready to intercept any other innuendo that may accompany this offensive word. Except for now baller is not offensive. Who knew? Apparently it is someone who is good at basketball or other sports.

Yo Mama: This is a widely used phrase that usually brings about good natured laughter, as in "Who borrowed my pen?" Then some 8th grader will holler out, "Yo mama."

Ain't nobody got time for that: OK, I teach grammar, but I know I can always say this one for a laugh. My students mentioned this ridiculous video on Youtube with the same title and, well, after watching it you may find yourself saying it too. Of course, since it was brought to my attention by 8th graders, I screened it. Yep, I couldn't show it because of inappropriate language. First rule of Youtube: screen it before showing kids!

Trolling: This was a great mystery to me until I looked it up on Urban Dictionary. The group of boys who frequently use this word (You are Trolling! Don't be a Troller!) couldn't or wouldn't explain the meaning beyond messing up someone else's video game. Trolling is basically being mean on the internet, something my generation never even had to imagine but kids today live with every moment. They don't even know how nice it all was before Facebook or cellphones…but that's another story.

Cool: I am so glad this is still…uh…cool. My dad says cool. I say cool. My 7th graders say cool. My 5-year old says cool. That's so cool.

Note: These are popular phrases today. The only thing I can guarantee is that these phrases will NOT be popular in a year. Remember **whatever, talk to the hand, the bomb**? **Groovy, neat** (which I still use all the time), **far out**? My protective technique, when it comes to slang, is to avoid using it all. Or to just stick with cool.

Oh, and the now not-so-popular phrase that earlier this fall seemed to be sweeping our school? **I'm going to punch you in the face**. Can you believe that? And not said in a threatening way, but usually said sweetly by a girl who would never, ever actually punch anyone in the face. I knew this was truly a slang term when my 8-year-old came home from her very nice school and kindly said she was going to punch someone in the face if she didn't have a snack soon.

Preschool

My children are both now in elementary school; no more preschool for us. I have to admit, I am grateful (extremely grateful) for our free public education. Now that I am no longer paying half my paycheck for my children to go to preschool and childcare I feel like a weight has been lifted. But I miss those preschool days. I miss the little notes home, the naps, the field trips to the fire department and the police station. I miss the creative art projects, all still taped up to the insides of all my cupboards and doors. I suppose I won't entirely miss the backpack full of papers and "drawings", full being the operative word. My children used to bring home so many pieces of paper each day that at times I felt I was drowning in them. I tried to tape up the special ones, moving previous masterpieces to the baby book. But after awhile the baby book became a baby box and soon I had so many pieces of art (many with just a single shaky line) I couldn't find room for them. I would have to sneak out, after the kids were asleep, and throw some things away. To ward off feelings of guilt, I would chant to myself, "It's the process, not the product." as I threw away their precious art.

I remember certain things about my own preschool days. Apparently I loved preschool (or more likely, my mom did!) because I attended multiple different programs: Betty Shields, the WWCC Parent Co-op, and Mary Drakes. I remember some of the songs we would sing, songs about the days of the week, songs about numbers, fun songs like the Farmer in the Dell. I remember Betty Shields bringing in a dentist who showed us plaster teeth and how to brush. I remember sharing my record player with my classmates at the Co-op. I was in my twenties before I realized most of the kids who attended Betty Shields with me also graduated from high school with me. Just another wonderful perk of growing up in a small town, knowing who used to suck their thumb and who cried when their mom left. Or in my case, who never brushed their hair and who insisted on being called Baby Chicago.

Walla Walla is so small I still regularly see most of the people in this photo.

I am the blonde (third from the right, middle row) who forgot to wear a dress.

My children were lucky enough to go to a pre-school called The Kids' Place. My Aunt Florene taught at Kids' Place when it was first founded and my younger brother, Daniel, was in one of the first groups. I was in high school at this time and I loved going to pick him up at school, seeing the quiet and organized groups of kids play with blocks and wear costumes. I decided at that point that my own children would attend The Kids' Place some day. Years later, when I found out I was expecting my first baby, I called Kids' Place to get put on the waiting list. The director thought nothing of putting a baby who was not expected to be born for 8 months on a waiting list. Good thing I did, too! Both of my kids even now still wish they could go.

Now that they are both in elementary school my life has opened up. Getting them to and from school is so easy with busing, they are pretty independent with their school work, and they only bring home the occasional art project. I love watching my kids grow up....though I do miss those preschool days.

Ethnic Food

When you have a large family meals look like this

Food has changed a lot since I was a kid, especially the availability of different types of ethnic food around Walla Walla. When I was little the only place we could go for anything remotely different from what mom made at home was The Modern for Chinese food. We certainly didn't eat Mexican food, Thai food, or anything else that veered too far from meat and potatoes. My dad would take me to the Modern on Fridays for lunch where I would always order the same thing: Pineapple Chicken and Fried Rice. Yum. To this day I still really like Pineapple Chicken, even though I prefer spicier and more vegetable-laden Chinese food now.

Really, though, Chinese food was easily the strangest thing anybody I knew ever ate. For food that was a little different we would go to Abby's Pizza (again, I always insisted on Pineapple, this time on the Hawaiian) or Merchants for a bagel and cream cheese.

Walla Walla continues to branch out in the food realm, Aloha Sushi is fantastic, Saffron and Pho Sho are delicious and elegant, Phoumy's is tasty. Brasserie Four has really interesting and appetizing food plus it caters nicely to little kids. But we can't give up our march toward out of the ordinary food offerings, maybe someday we will even have an Indian food restaurant. And Mexican food. How did I ever live without Mexican food? Yes, I lived in Mexico for two years as a young adult, I am a Spanish teacher, so I may be a little biased....but I loooooove Mexican food. I eat Mexican food probably three times a week and it is my favorite choice if faced with a varied menu. Clarettes? The Mexican-style omelette. Bacon and Eggs? The huevos rancheros. The Brew Pub? The spicy hamburger. The Green? Fish Tacos. I remember when most of us didn't even know what Mexican food was. We had Outrageous Taco on Main street where you could get a really good burrito. And....that was it. No tortas or guacamole or taquitos or chiles rellenos. How did we survive? And remember the days when we didn't even have taco trucks? I remember the first one I went to in Walla Walla, it is still there, parked at Melody Muffler, Taco Loco. Oh yum. I think I need to take a little break and go buy a torta from there right now. Be right back. Hands down, though, my favorite is Taqueria Jungapeti, mainly because of their salsa selection and the pans of warm chiles and onions. I eat there at least once a week, rotating between the torta and the taco plate, both of the Walla Walla variety which means they include avocado and caramelized onions.

My dad told me when he was a boy food was even less varied than now. His family ate different variations of beef, pork, or chicken with a side of potatoes and a vegetable every evening. He chuckled as he described the first time his mom ventured out and made an Italian food called "spaghetti", a foreign noodle dish she fried in tomatoes. It looked nothing like the spaghetti we eat once or twice a week now! She discovered the recipe by talking to friends, Mexican-Americans from Texas who occasionally worked with our family on their strawberry farm in the 1940's. When my dad visited his first Italian restaurant in the

1960's he ordered the only item he had heard of before, spaghetti. He could barely choke it down. It was quite different from the delicious, crunchy spaghetti his mom would prepare. This Italian stuff was slimy and he could barely swallow it.

My dad also likes to tell the story of the time as a young man he attempted to make a French dish, Quiche Lorraine. He and my mom both really liked it, enough to order it on a trip to a fancy restaurant in Portland. My mom doesn't like this part of the story, though, because when she ordered, the waiter snickered at her pronunciation of quiche as 'quick'. Oh well, we can't all be sophisticated and worldly. In fact, just last week my boyfriend, Paul, kindly told me that when I had been espousing the benefits of the sparkling water 'PerriER' it is actually pronounced Pear-e-AY. Ooo-la-la.

Fiesta!

Quiche Lorraine

Quiche Lorraine
Recipe courtesy Greg Van Donge
It is pronounced 'keesh low-**rayne**'

A baked pie crust

Saute   1/4 pound bacon to tender not crisp

Custard:
Mix   2 Cups Cream
                3 Eggs
                1/4 Tsp Salt
                1/8 Tsp Pepper
                1/8 Tsp Pepper
                (1 Tsp Chopped Chives)
                1/2 Cup Swiss Cheese, grated

To Assemble:

Place bacon in layer on pie crust, followed by cheese. Pour over custard mixture. (You can moisture-proof your pie crust by brushing on egg yolk while cooling) Bake in 375 oven for 35 - 40 minutes.

Fried Spaghetti

Fried Spaghetti
Also known as Fideo con Carne

Ingredients

> 3 Tablespoons Olive Oil
> 1 Pound Beef Shoulder, cut into 1/4-inch cubes
> (or substitute Ground Beef)
> 1/2 Onion, chopped
> 2 Garlic Cloves, minced
> 15 Chile Pequins or 2 Jalapeños, chopped
> 1 15-oz Can Tomato Sauce
> 1 Tablespoon Homemade Chili Powder
> 1 Teaspoon Dried Mexican Oregano
> 5 - 7 ounces Fideo (Mexican-Style Pasta)

Directions

Heat 2 tablespoons of the oil in a large skillet of medium-high heat. Add the mean and brown on all sides about 5 minutes. Add the onion, garlic, and chiles. Continue cooking for 5 to 7 minutes or until the onion is soft. Add the tomato sauce, the chili powder, ad the oregano and stir well. Reduce to a simmer.

Heat the remaining tablespoon oil in a skillet over medium-high heat. Add the fideo to the skillet and stir until nicely browned, about 5 minutes.

Combine the browned video and the mean mixture. Add the 1/2 cup water and stir well. Cover and simmer for 5 minutes, stirring ofter, until the fideo is soft. Add more water if the mixture becomes too dry. Serve immediately.

Tapatio

Greg: Mr. Tapatio

Tapatio has a prominent place in my kitchen, a place of honor on the table held by no other item. Even salt, pepper, and butter have taken a back seat to my favorite food addition. My kids would probably argue that ketchup is more important than Tapatio, but I have to disagree. Nothing else gives food that special kick.

But I remember the days when I didn't even know what Tapatío was. Sure, I had heard of Tabasco, Tapatío's less tasty cousin, but I didn't really eat it. I was in high school when I first discovered the joys of suffering through extremely spicy food. It started with my first boyfriend, Pablo and his family. A shared love of The Cure and Tennis brought us together, though our biggest enjoyment was thrift store shopping. The first time I went to Pablo's house his Aunt Irma immediately offered me a snack. Never one to turn down food, I accepted. I remember clearly sitting down to their cheerful table and seeing they were eating cucumber doused in Tapatío, lime juice, and salt. I was a little dubious at first; I had never considered putting anything on cucumbers. In fact, I doubt I had ever willingly eaten cucumbers before.

But I am adventurous when it comes to food and I tried it. Besides the obvious burning of the chili, the Tapatío-covered cucumbers were wonderful! What a surprise! But not as big a surprise as the other things these guys ate with Tapatío: watermelon, hot dogs, pizza, peanuts.... In fact, later when I traveled to Mexico to go to college, I discovered that Tapatío was so ubiquitous that running out was reason to run to the store before a meal. Even at the elegant discos and clubs I would visit with my friends we could count on popcorn sprinkled with Tapatío to be offered at every table. Imagine? All dressed up, sitting in a very fancy and exclusive nightclub, eating Tapatío-coated popcorn? What a culture shock!

I lived with a family while in Mexico and they loved Tapatío so much they would take a knife to the small hole at the top and cut it open a bit further so the spicy hot sauce could come out just that much faster. This was a big bottle, mind you, not a child-size mini-bottle. Now I also have a big bottle of Tapatío at my own house, I'm not sure how I ever lived without it.

My favorite thing about Tapatío, though, is how my dad, Greg seems to have been the model for the Tapatío guy. I never noticed before my son, Noah, pointed it out. Noah was about three when we were eating breakfast, the giant Tapatío bottle strategically placed near my right hand.

"Grampa!" Noah shouted, pointing.

I looked all around, but saw no sign of my dad coming up the front walk.

"Where, Noah?" I asked.

"Right there!" Noah hollered, pointing at the guy on the Tapatio bottle.

Sure enough, there was my dad, smiling out from the bottle. Everyone was pretty entertained when we pointed this out to him, and my dad is pretty good natured when we tease him about it every time we see the Tapatio bottle. Oh yeah, that's at every meal.

Dogs Vs. Cats

I realize I write about dogs a lot. I really like dogs, even though I do not currently get to own one. I'll admit I am partial to them, the ready wag of the tail, the exuberant eagerness to go on walks, the agreeable greetings. I wouldn't want anyone to think I don't like cats, though, so at the urging of our family friend, Lois, I will write about how great cats are. Or I'll try.

I'm allergic to cats. This is the main reason I don't have a lot to say about them. I get all stuffy and itchy and wheezy even being in the same room with a cat. In fact, I can enter someone's house and tell if there is a cat within fifteen minutes, even if I never actually see the cat. People sometimes try to help me out by vacuuming and dusting their houses to rid them of the cat fur, but this only seems to make it worse, I think because the dander gets pushed into the air.

As a child I used to think this allergy could go away. I would wait a few months between trying to pet a cat and then I would think I had gotten over it. I would then grab a cat and press my face into it's fur. Did it go away? Not at all. I would then spend the rest of the day covered in hives, itching my eyes and wheezing.

Despite my body completely rejecting cats, I really like them. Usually. Sure, there are those weird cats that act like they want you to pet them but then latch onto your arm with their sharp claws once you try. Or the cats who just hiss and run away. I suppose these cats probably have some kind of psychological problem, they can be sub-categorized into the same classification as annoying or mean dogs. Not representative of all cats, just anomalies that make the rest of the species look bad.

When I was a little kid we had a cat named Pepper. He was a big, talkative Siamese cat. Pepper was pretty friendly, in fact I remember he didn't even get that mad at me when I was very little and tried to pull one of the pads off his foot because I thought it was a chocolate chip. Pepper was friendly with the whole neighborhood, a fact that eventually cost him his freedom. We had a neighbor who had a little dog with his own dog door. Pepper liked to sneak into this lady's house and eat that poor little dog's food. The lady didn't appreciate our cat breaking into her house, so one day she took Pepper to the Pound where he was promptly adopted by someone new. Or so they say. I wonder now if maybe this whole story might not just have been made up to appease me when Pepper died.

There was another notable neighborhood cat when I was a kid, this one may even have been more distinctive than our thieving Pepper. This cat had owners who shaved him each summer. I know they were probably being kind, but the cat looked like a lion and it was so ridiculous we would go out of our way to look for it and laugh at it. Poor cat, he probably developed some kind of issue from having my brother and cousins and me pointing, doubled-up, laughing at him. In fact, that cat could have ended up being one of those mean hiss and claw cats later, who could blame him?

Incidentally, if I were to read this aloud in the room with any dog I have ever owned, the frequency with which I say the word cat would probably cause the poor canine to have a minor seizure. Try it. See what happens to your dog right now if you read this aloud, does he go nuts? Is he looking around for the cat? See? Dogs are just plain entertaining. If you read an article about dogs aloud in the company of cats the cat would just glare at you and flounce out of the room. This may be the biggest difference between dogs and cats: exuberance (or is that intelligence?) Either way, both types of animals have their merits, I'm glad we get to have them around.

Christmas

It just doesn't get as cold as it used to. Ok I'm not really sure if that is true, but enough people say it and it really does seem true - I remember winter being a little snowier when I was a little girl. When I was 8, about 1984, we had a big snow storm - similar to the one in 2009. But, I remember it rained on top of it. Then froze. So we had calf-deep snow, crusted on top with ice. I was small enough to walk on it but it would break on occasion, cutting my ankles. Now that is Christmas weather.

I've made the decision to slow it down this holiday season so my family and I can really enjoy Christmas. As a young adult it seemed December was one Christmas party after another, it was fun but got a little exhausting. And as a little kid, Christmas was amazing and magical – snow angels, stockings full of candy and oranges, secret Santa's at school, presents under the tree. My parents made the most delicious date-filled cookies, they were like little pies. My dad and my aunt Debbie both still continue to make my great-aunt Mable Gable's Christmas spice cake with chocolate chips (yes, Mable Gable. My dad likes to joke she turned down a Mr. Syrup to marry my great Uncle Gable). And Christmas Eve was so fun! We would go to my great grandparent's house for dinner where we kids were relegated to the kitchen to sit at the kids' table. Afterwards we went to church where I remember singing Silent Night in German as we lit candles. Though we no longer sing in German at Christ Lutheran, we still sing Silent Night with candles. I love that, it seems like one of the few moments during the whole season where it actually seems to still feel like Christmas. While we were in church Santa would deliver the presents to my grandparent's house, ready for the hurricane of gift opening when we returned. There were so many cousins, so many gifs, and so much wrapping paper that some new toy or other would inevitably get lost in the fray. It was delightful chaos.

A few times the party got to be pretty big, my Nanny and Fafa really enjoyed a good party; one year they put all of us kids into the back bedroom and told us it was time to go to sleep. I'm sure the adults thought we would go to sleep, but we had other ideas. We started jumping on the bed, eventually jumping so much the whole thing broke and landed on the floor. I think I remember my mom taking us home about this point. I guess it's not a real Christmas party until the furniture starts breaking.

Christmas Day was always more subdued (after the party the night before, who could blame them?). My brother and I would head off to my dad's for more presents, breakfast, then another large food-filled party. My childhood Christmases were full of love and not a little excitement, that's hard to beat today.

I admit the magic of Christmas has gradually faded as I've gotten older, in fact I've had a couple of sad, solitary Christmases when my kids were with their dad and my parents were working. Thank goodness for my friends who were kind enough to invite me to spend the holiday with their families. Now the magic lies in making it special for my own kids by getting the tree lit up and decorated, listening to Christmas music, and wrapping presents. Plus the movies! The Grinch, Christmas Vacation, It's a Wonderful Life, and – my favorite, mainly because I love Bing Crosby's voice – White Christmas. A very special tradition my kids and I have is reading Christmas books, we love Polar Express, Best Christmas Pageant Ever, Santa Calls, well, all of them, because they really make it seem like Christmas has arrived. We have other traditions too, my daughter helps me hide a 'Santa on the Shelf' each evening for her little brother to find when he wakes up in the morning. She is also looking forward to helping me play Santa Clause this Christmas Eve – I guess that's one good thing about discovering Mom is really Santa, a fact she figured out by noticing the gifts from me and the gifts from Santa all had wrapping paper from Inland Octopus. She may be a little too smart for her own good!

Now my family seems to have grown smaller. My children have far fewer cousins than I had, in fact none of my 5 siblings even has a family. Hmmmmm.... maybe that is the solution, marry some of those guys off.... oh, I digress. But our holiday is no longer an enormous family dinner followed by a raging community party followed by a second enormous family dinner. Or maybe it is. Maybe from my childhood perspective the dinners and parties just seemed gigantic because I was still young enough to be blessed with that magical feeling of Christmas. Despite the smaller size and calmer weather, I am still looking forward to a happy holiday with my family. Being on the mom side of things is different, I no longer expect any gifts and instead it is all about what I will get for my children. I am no longer relegated to a kitchen table so adults can talk – but I still get to help cook and clean up. And, hey, who knows, maybe we'll get really lucky this year and get a foot of ice-crusted snow!

Natalie playing Christmas carols on the ukelele

Christmas Cake

Christmas Cake
Originally called Applesauce Chocolate Nugget Loaf
Courtesy Mable Gable

Ingredients

3 1/2 Cups Flour
2 Tsp Baking Soda
1/2 Tsp Salt
1/2 Tsp Ground Cloves
2 Tsp Cinnamon
1 Cup Butter, unsalted
2 Cups Sugar
4 Eggs, un-beaten
2 Cups Applesauce
1/2 Cup Raisins
1/2 Cup Chopped Dates
1 Cup Chopped Pecans or Walnuts
2 Cups Bittersweet Chocolate Chips

Directions

Sift together flour, soda, salt and spices. Cream butter, add sugar gradually and cream until light and fluffy. Add eggs one at a time, beating well after each addition, until smooth. Stir in raisins, dates, nuts, and chocolate chips.

Pour batter into 9"x5"x3" loaf pans which have been greased and floured on bottom. Bake at 325 for 90 minutes.

Winter Gloves

The cold is here. I keep trying to find things to enjoy about our extreme cold weather, I may as well learn to love it since winter has only just begun and we still have until mid-March before any hope of warm weather returning. I do enjoy any excuse to sit in front of the fireplace and read or watch a movie, cold weather meals in the crock pot are always a treat to come home to, and I have a lot of really beautiful cold weather clothing that I love to put on each year as it cools down. But dressing my own children for the cold has never been easy, and for my son, now that he no longer has his teachers at Educare and Assumption Preschool to help remind him to find his hat and gloves and scarves, cold weather gear has become a daily struggle. We can't seem to keep gloves around, especially little boy gloves. Curse the makers of gender-specific clothing! Boots with characters on them or pink or purple gloves, now totally useless to a boy sensitive to the possibility of ridicule for wearing "girl" clothes. How sad is it that someone would rather go to school when it is three degrees outside wearing no gloves over pink gloves because his green gloves were stolen at Macys? Sad.

Luckily my mom gave us my younger brother Mason's gloves. Now I am watching my son's only gloves like a hawk. Every morning there is a small panic as we dress and every afternoon the tiny thrill of fear as they get off the bus. "Do you have the gloves? The gloves, are they in your pocket??!" My friend Kim said they have a similar glove situation going on at her house. Where do all these missing gloves go? Actually, I may have an idea; a pair of hot pink stretchy gloves has been sitting, unclaimed, on the edge of my desk at work for over a week. No middle schooler will claim them. Obviously no boy wants them, but surely some girl walked into my class wearing them one of these many below-freezing mornings. Now her mother is probably trying to get her to wear some ugly boy gloves as she goes around bare-handed, freezing rather than risk looking unattractive.

But we endure the cold because we know winter will end. Spring wouldn't give us that same thrill if we didn't have to slough through miserable ice and cold and darkness for three months. Spring wouldn't make our hearts fill with joy and delight, each blossoming flower and twittering bird causing us to beam, if we didn't have to look outside day after day and see nothing but still gray. It is worth it. Even though it is still months away and somehow I am already suffering I know spring will come, this makes it all worthwhile, even the possibility of having to wear ugly gloves.

Streets

Main Street, 1953, before all trees and planting strip were removed

I love narrow winding streets. I hope no one gets annoyed with me because of this statement, because my love of picturesque streets, lined with trees, isn't necessarily a popular opinion. I know people like to drive quickly, efficiently, and safely down wide streets. I know parking on the street, in front of our houses, is much easier than trying to squeeze into driveways or parking in alleys. I know when driving down a really narrow street it can be frustrating and even scary to have to take turns passing or go 10 miles per hour. I am practical, I do tend to take 9th and

Isaacs, large busy streets and I appreciate their width, but I wonder what Walla Walla was like before street expansion.

My mom, Linda, talks about streets like Isaacs Avenue before it was widened. Did you know Isaacs used to be a narrow, tree-lined street? Imagine! She said Isaacs Avenue was pretty. I remember before a street called Wilbur was widened in the late 1980's, it was also narrower and had more trees. At the time the street was widened the people with houses on Wilbur lost large areas out of their front yards. Even as a young child I wondered about the logic in this. I'm sure there are many excellent, practical arguments for nice wide streets, but for a romantic like me I tend to admire beauty more than practicality. I guess our world needs all sorts of people to keep a good balance.

Another type of street we see here in Walla Walla is the car-friendly yet attractive variety such as the ones found on the South side of town. At one point I owned a lovely home on Hillbrooke Drive near Tietan Park. Our house was built in 1955 and the street represents the sentiment of that era – no sidewalks, winding and pretty, wide and practical. I remember in my college geography class our professor at Eastern Oregon University, Dr. Lewis, would show us slide shows and yell out sociology terms. One of his favorites was "Auto-Air Amenity Era!" while flashing a picture of a car-oriented society. Our street on Hillbrooke would have been a perfect picture for the concept. Even though the winding streets of the older parts of the South side of town are pretty, I still prefer the oldest parts of town where the streets have parking strips and sidewalks. My absolute favorite street to walk down is Palouse, not only is the street tree-lined and quiet, but the houses are fabulous.

When I see the new developments popping up around town I am really pleased to see a smart combination of all the practical and attractive ideas from the past. I really like the street design in the Provenance Housing Development near the Community College. The streets are rounded and have sidewalks and trees, it is attractive and encourages people to slow down and walk. And really, what are streets and sidewalks for? To travel, right? So if we look at how the streets around us are designed, we can see what our community values. I am happy to see our community veering more toward walking and beauty, I am reassured by the positive growth of Walla Walla.

Chickens

My mom, Linda, recently got chickens. I never really saw my mom as the trendy sort, so when she excitedly called up to say she had inherited a friend's chickens, I had to chuckle. You see, chickens have become this cool thing to do, right up there with eating organic food and recycling and riding a bike. All the stuff that made me a total weirdo in Chicago back in the late 1990's are now the quickest route to being hip here in the Pacific Northwest. Oh yes, the requisite heavy black glasses and posting food pictures on social media sites are also a must.

But chickens lead the parade. Of course, no one really likes to think about the realities of chickens, the extreme excrement exploding exclusively around your yard, or how they scratch and pick that same yard to shreds, or how other animals like possums and raccoons will sometimes sneak in and eat them in the night. Or how they sometimes eat their own eggs, and if they are anything like my mom's Marge, a striped Americana, once they start this they never stop. Once a self-egg eater, always a self-egg eater, I guess.

But I digress, my mom loves her chickens, I sometimes feel a little jealous, like she might like them better than my kids. She raves about them on Facebook, regales us with stories about them when we're at family parties, and was ecstatic when their picture came out in the newspaper.

But a few weeks ago one disappeared. My mom lets the chickens out most days so they can cluck around freely, getting delicious grubs and seeds or whatever it is they are doing. Plus poop on her porch. And they are really cute, they are big and fluffy, Danni and Parker are identical, both black and white Plymouth Rocks. But this evening when my mom rattled the popcorn box to get the chickens to come a-running in, Danni (who is also the best layer) did not come home. My mom looked all over the yard with a flashlight but never could find her.

She was so worried she called me the next day to tell me about it, then she drove around town to see if she could see Danni hopping down Main street, I guess. My mom lives right downtown (I know, that may be the best part of this story. She has chickens right downtown), so as she was at one of the busier intersections waiting for the light to turn green she saw her little sister Janet. Linda rolled down the window and hollered at her sister that her chicken was missing, to keep an eye out for it, before driving away. I know we are supposed to be a sophisticated tourist town, but what would our fine visitors think about an exchange like this? Maybe they would just think they had tasted too much wine.

Thankfully, later that afternoon my mom mentioned the tragedy to her paper carrier, the slender blonde one who has delivered forever, and the carrier said she would also keep her eyes open. Chalk another one up for having a positive outlook! This is why my mom's life often seems to go so well, she always expects the best and lo! it happens. Apparently a green-haired young man a few blocks over had a chicken spend the previous night on his front porch and wasn't sure where it had come from, so when the paper carrier mentioned the missing chicken to him he did his neighborly duty and drove over to my mom's. I have to add here how interesting it is that everyone here is driving when they could easily walk, but that is another story.

So it was all nicely resolved, he rang Linda's doorbell, she walked over to his house (which was across two very busy streets, that Danni is a brave one!) and was able to retrieve her baby and bring her home. Good thing too, it was very cold that night and nobody, not even a chicken, should have to sleep out in the cold. It was funny, too, because as she walked home a couple of Whitman College students saw her and asked her if she was carrying a real chicken!

After all this excitement I think maybe I should get some chickens.

Breakfast

I like to say I have never skipped breakfast, never in my entire life. When I was in high school I had a teacher ask our class who ate breakfast. Only two of us raised our hands, my friend Afton and me. I remember being surprised, it had not occurred to me before this time that other people didn't eat breakfast. Sure, I had heard teachers lecture us about the importance of breakfast, but I had always figured they were just talking to talk, I didn't think there were people who actually set out into the world each day without eating. That would be crazy.

And I didn't just eat cereal. My dad would make us a fabulous breakfast every morning, he would cook up something sweet and something savory, usually something like blueberry pancakes and potatoes with caramelized onions. Or oatmeal and sausage. Or toast and eggs. My brother Christian and I would stumble out into the kitchen before school and my dad would cheerfully hand us our breakfast, humming and telling us to be cool at school. We were ungrateful teenagers who would grumble about having to eat and running late, but we knew how lucky we were to get real maple syrup and a hot breakfast pushed under our noses at 7:00 every morning.

One of our favorite stories, OK, my favorite, definitely not Christians, is the time Chris ate weevils. One morning when I was in junior high I got to the kitchen a few minutes after Chris, by the time I got there he was already wolfing down his oatmeal. I looked closely at my own oatmeal and noticed it looked funny, in fact - were those weevils? I pointed them out to my dad who tried to stop the hungry Chris, but it was no use, my brother had already eaten an entire bowl full of the little creatures. Chris tried to make himself sick, but he wasn't even able to do that, he just had to live with the fact that he'd eaten a bowl of weevils for breakfast.

I make breakfast for my own family today too. I love breakfast, it is my favorite meal of the day. I have a small repertoire I move through: oatmeal; eggs, toast and bacon; blueberry crepes; smoothies; granola with fruit and yogurt. My kids often request Cream of Wheat, pancakes, and waffles, but these are not breakfast foods that I enjoy so I only make them on weekends when I have time to make two separate breakfasts. I also never make my dad's specialty, his potatoes and onions, because they also take to long and I just haven't been able to make them taste as good as his always do.

Sometimes we go out to breakfast, Walla Walla has so many options for my favorite meal, from fancy to homestyle. As a child my family and I would go to Perkins Pancake House, now Clarettes, near Whitman College where I would order a Li'l Cowpoke. Today my family and I still love Clarettes for the friendly service, solid breakfasts, and comfortable atmosphere. My children don't get to order a Li'l Cowpoke, but the ultra-sweet smiley-face pancake seems to be a good substitute.

Being Walla Walla, though, it seems easier to find fancy breakfast places. Bacon and Eggs is a hip re-designed former gas station with fancy adult beverages and creative and healthy food. My dad loves going there, so sometimes we take the kids. I've discover that, even though they have a long line on Sunday mornings, if I am alone when the kids are visiting their dad I can go in by myself and sit at the counter and it is a good place to pass the time while I wait for my family to come home.

Walla Walla may have a fancy veneer, but we can't forget our humble origins. I love that my hometown has turned into a tourist town, it makes me happy every time a new magazine mentions Walla Walla or whenever I see people here visiting on vacation. But those of us that are from here like to go home to old familiar places too. One is Tommy's Dutch Lunch, a place you can't judge by its appearance! Tommy's is on the old highway surrounded by run-down businesses, chain-link fences, and parking lots, but the food is amazing and the service top notch. At Tommy's you can enjoy large portions and great selection while surrounded by true Walla Wallans. As an added bonus, the power station directly behind Tommy's provides power even during the roughest power outage. A few years ago when we had a terrible wind storm. The wind was blowing so hard that fences were blowing over, trees were falling and the power was out all over town. My mom and I had planned on going to the grocery store together while my kids were with their dad for two hours, but by the time she got to my house every business in town was without electricity. Every business but Tommy's. We didn't want to sit in the cold dark house so we joined the throngs of people waiting in the tiny lobby, but my mom, being a true old-school Walla Wallan, didn't hesitate to ask a table with two vacant seats if we could join them. Of course we immediately established a small town connection and all enjoyed each other's company while we took shelter from the storm.

Christian (happy not to be eating weevils) and Sara

Crepes

Crepes

Ingredients
4 Eggs
1/4 Cup Milk
2 Tablespoons Flour
2 Tablespoons Butter

Heat a mid-size skillet to medium heat.
Whisk together eggs, milk, and flour until smooth.
Melt 1 teaspoon butter, add 1/4 cup crepe batter, lifting the pan to cover the bottom. Heat 1-3 minutes until the sides start to lift and the crepe can be turned easily. Flip and heat 30 seconds more.

Servings: 4

Optional Toppings:
Maple Syrup
Fruit
Yogurt

Sara Van Donge

Packing

Summertime is coming and with it maybe some vacation time. For me, one of the hardest parts about traveling is packing. For some reason I have never been a great packer, maybe it is my laissez faire attitude about life: it will work out I'm sure! But I can't count the trips I've been on where I show up without important items: socks, shoes, shampoo. Or the times I pack the right clothing but for the wrong weather. Or the right clothing but for the wrong occasion. Maybe this is just a subliminal excuse to buy myself something new when I go on vacation. Or maybe it's just a way for me to make the vacation more exciting for everyone involved.

Probably the best example is the time when I took my kids to Bend to visit their grandparents. It was July so they wouldn't really need much, maybe a couple pairs of shorts, some underclothes, a pair of pajamas and a swimsuit. What could go wrong? At the time they were four and six and I thought they were old enough to understand how to pack for themselves. I gave each of them a small backpack and looked them right in the eyes and told them exactly what to get. Then I made extra sure they understood by asking them to repeat to me so I could be sure they really understood. Then they ran to their rooms and packed while I put sleeping bags and pillows and our ice chest in the car. When they came bumping down the stairs with their bags, all proud at having packed themselves, I asked again - you have shorts? Underwear? Pajamas? A swimsuit? They nodded and promised they did. So we grabbed our bags and hopped in our car and drove to Bend.

Did they have their necessary things? Well, half of them did. My six year old was indeed ready to pack for herself, she had everything I had told her to bring plus about five extra outfits - the lifetime over-packer was already visible beneath her sweet little six-year old exterior. But my four year old? No. Did Noah bring shorts or t-shirts or underwear? Nah, who needs those silly things? No, Noah brought one thing: his puffy Spiderman suit, one of those that look like the kid has muscles when they wear it. It was so big with the fake muscles it took up the whole bag. Needless to say we had to make a little trip to the store; Noah probably needed new clothes anyway.

Spiderman likes to go on vacation too

Misters

Relaxing in the backyard

Wet towels. Fans. Frozen hot water bottles. What do these things have in common? They are the lifelines for those of us trying to keep cool without air conditioning. As a child I grew up in a home without air conditioning and I am well-versed in the work required in surviving summertime in Walla Walla without it. Waking up very early in the morning to make sure all the doors and windows are closed at that precise moment when it is hotter outdoors than indoors. Keeping a full water bottle in the freezer to sleep with because who doesn't sleep better with a large frozen sheep between their knees? Keeping all the shades and curtains drawn all day. Praying for rain. And my new favorite remedy: misters!

Now I'm not saying Misters, like Mr. A and Mr. B, I am saying misters like the little sprinklers that spray tiny droplets of water around your head when you are outside. What a brilliant idea! I can't remember, exactly, when I first noticed misters, but I don't remember them being around when I was younger. Now they are ubiquitous. No outdoor restaurant or garden center or even home patio is complete without them.

I recently managed to track down and install misters in my own backyard. It was the fifth day of over 100 degree weather here in scorching Walla Walla in the middle of July and I realized none of us wanted to leave the house unless it was after 9:00 at night. I had been to a party the previous weekend and our hostess had a free-standing mister that she pointed at us as we sat on the deck. I was struck with the overwhelming realization that I needed a mister. Now!

I'm not usually much of a shopper. For some reason, stores make me anxious. I think it is the vast amount of stuff that I either A) don't need, B) do need but can't afford or C) can neither need nor afford yet still want. Somehow this cascade of wanting and needing makes me feel like I must flee quickly before I buy something I don't have room for in my garage. But on this 104 degree scorcher of a mid-July day I dragged my kids around town in search of the ever-more elusive mister. I went to the obvious places first, Home Depot, Shopko, and BiMart. When these had no misters (are they crazy?) I even ventured as far as the Wal-Mart parking lot. I refused to go in, though, I had reached my absolute threshold and Wal-Mart is the ultimate in torture for a non-shopper like me. At Wal-Mart I pulled up next to the garden center and called in to the extremely kind greeter lady to ask if they had misters. She didn't think I was crazy (or at least didn't let on that she thought I was crazy) when I wouldn't go in, she even walked to the door to talk to me. And not even Wal-Mart had misters. Unbelievable.

Trying not to let discouragement completely overtake me, I started calling around. In the middle of this one of my friends sent me a text saying her boss, Tom Macaroni, had just purchased three misters for TMacs at Ace Hardware and there was one left. I started hollering like a rebel on the warpath to my kids to quick get back in the car, Tom Macaroni had found misters and by golly I was going to find one too! I ran into Ace a few minutes later and managed to buy two. None of their employees seemed as frantic as I was about the whole situation, but none of them had unsuccessfully been to four other stores either. When I returned home, triumphant, with my misters my kids finally understood why I had been so determined to buy these sprinklers that hang from the ceiling.

Now we are able to enjoy our backyard, especially because while we were at Ace, Noah spotted a tiny blue plastic swimming pool, which I also purchased to replace our old broken one. Our backyard is now a mecca! We can happily pass away an entire afternoon splashing and relaxing thanks to Ace Hardware. I think I can avoid going to stores for quite awhile, maybe until school starts. Too bad I can't sleep with the misters above my bed.

And no, I did not get paid by Ace Hardware or the misters union to write this. Though maybe I should!

Shoes

My favorite shoes died. I had to finally throw them away and I really miss them. They were silver wedge Jambu sandals with an ankle strap and really good traction. I bought them a year ago and have worn them at least four times a week since. I wore them to Disneyland last summer, walking at least eight hours each day with never even the slightest annoyance. My number one priority with shoes is that they be cute. Ooooops. I mean that they be comfortable. Yes, that they be comfortable. So when I find a pair that are comfortable and actually cute, I cling to them.

These shoes wore out peacefully enough, first wearing through the sole in patches, then beginning to lose individual straps. It wasn't until I wore them camping, though, that they really gave in. I happened to be wearing them for travel, I had brought along another pair of practical shoes for the actual camping. However, being me, I took the practical shoes off after an hour - they got wet in the river - and then promptly lost them. I did manage to find them under our tent when we packed up three days later, but by this point my comfortable and cute silver sandals were destroyed. They did hold out for various hikes from the cabin to the river, but it was wading through the river that did them in. They gave their all and lived a very honorable life, I'm happy I was able to enjoy them as long as I did.

I've had other shoes wear out, some I was able to just replace, others I took to Saagers Shoes in Milton-Freewater for repair. The shoe repair people at Saagers are practically miracle workers. I found two pairs of fabulous (and, yes, comfortable) wedge heel sandals at an estate sale about 10 years ago. They are from an Italian company called Famolare and are the Hi There style, one is navy blue and the other is a light brown. I love these shoes. Love. I wear them everywhere and can walk in them comfortably, plus they are stylish and look good with everything. I read on a recent search online that the Famolare company is out of business, not to mention a pair like mine are for sale on Ebay for over one hundred dollars. Wow. I'm tempted to just leave them on display in my closet now. Thanks to Saagers shoes I was able to get them resoled the two times they started to show some wear. Did I mention I love those shoes?

I have worn other items of clothing to death. Is this a family trait? We find one item of clothing and wear it ad naseum until it disintegrates? My younger brother, Daniel, has been known to wear clothes out too. There's a Misfits shirt I won't mention. And a gray sweat suit. A pair of blue moon boots. But I'll let Daniel off the hook. When I was in my early twenties I found a cashmere cardigan, robins egg blue, at an estate sale (the same one as the shoes, I think the name was Snyder, classy lady). I wore that poor sweater to shreds. It started with a small hole at the wrist, then the elbow, then a larger one in the arm pit. Eventually the sweater just disappeared. I tried to cling to it, eventually pulling a similar black cashmere cardigan over the top of it, making it a holy liner. But the beautiful blue cardigan just could not endure the endless wearing and washing, and today all that remains are some mother of pearl buttons and one small swatch of material. I still miss you sweater.

My own children do not wear clothes or shoes out, they seem to enjoy variety in dressing much more than I do. My son usually has some type of costume going - he rotates between being a pirate, a ninja, and a variety of different superheroes. My daughter, surely only to prevent wear on her clothes, changes outfits about five times a day. She has an affinity for elaborately decorated tops and dresses, the more sparkle and lace, the better. Me? I still wear clothes out. As I write this I can feel a little breeze blowing through the hole in the armpit of my favorite pink sweater, I guess this means I may need to retire this one too.

Noah found this suit at a thrift store, it is now his favorite outfit

Shorts

When I posted this picture of my family in Disneyland on Facebook, what did everyone comment on? Not the 3-D glasses. Not how much fun we were having. Not even asking where we were. No, everyone wanted to know why 16-year old Hannah is dressed in those short-shorts while the rest of us look like we're ready for a winter storm. My answer? If you can wear shorts like this, you better be wearing them because the time is brief. If you've got it, flaunt it!

Shorts. As a teenager I never, ever imagined shorts would be a problem. But now that I'm an adult summer has come with a certain dread – the dread of shorts. Now please do not think I am in any way complaining about my strong, healthy body. Not at all. I am thankful for my legs that carry me anywhere I need to go….it is shorts that I am annoyed with.

It used to be swimsuits. Going to the store at the end of spring to shiver around in a harshly lit dressing room would be miserable even for a tall, skinny supermodel. For an average-sized woman like me it is so terrible I decided at the young age of 25 to simply never do it again. A few years ago in a fit of anxiety about the horror of finding a comfortable semi-flattering swimsuit, I went to Goodwill and bought as many different swimsuits as I could find. I brought them home and I actually found one that doesn't make me feel like something is wrong with me. What a triumph! Thankfully I rarely wear a swimsuit anymore, so I will probably own this one for many more years.

But now it is shorts. What happens when manufacturers make shorts? I go to the Y in the morning, I walk, I do yoga, I eat breakfast and drink water. I'm lucky enough to be in fairly good shape – not like I'm going to make money off my looks, but acceptable. Yet…shorts are this nightmare situation to find. They gape and cling and hurt and are too long or too short or too tight. Or a horrifying mixture of all these things. I would rather wear a swimsuit bottom and a long shirt than shorts. Oh, I guess that's like just not wearing anything at all, so scratch that, maybe I will just not wear shorts at all, ever again. Is that an ok thing?

About two years ago I couldn't find any to wear, at any store. I ended up spending way too much on a pair of Calvin Klein jean shorts at Macys that sort of fit, they at least didn't hurt. But after washing them once they shrunk or something so the tops of the white pockets stuck out and the little legs rode up and I kept having to pull them down. They were horrible. This was about the point when I banned shorts from my life forever. And Calvin Klein. And clothes from Macys.

Shopping for clothes can be a nightmare; if it's not your size it's your income, if it's not your income it's not being able to find anything. I have never been a woman who enjoys shopping for clothes. I guess this is why when I find something I tend to buy two or even three. Then I'm off the hook for shopping for a long, long time.

Now here's a swimsuit I might actually like - and only $6.50!!

Camping

My family and I have always enjoyed camping, from rustic tent camping, hearty backpacking trips, easy car camping and near-camping in cabins. I'm thankful I learned how to camp as a child because now I can take my own children camping. One of our favorite places is the Lewis and Clark campground between Dayton and Waitsburg. The highlight of the trip for my children was the river, a joyful experience soon stopped by my fear of someone getting swept downstream. But for the few minutes they had to enjoy the swift current of the Touchet River they were thrilled. I can't say I blame them, they joined another group of children (who had a much more laid-back mom, she chatted happily on her cell phone while her three small children courted death - I mean played in the water). The kids had discovered a section of the river where they could jump from the bank into a current which carried them about ten feet down to a place they could pull themselves out and do it all over again.

My kids, who make up for a lack of swimming skills with confidence, jumped in before I had a chance to investigate. By the time I made my way to them, my 8-year-old daughter was already a near expert at the feat. 6-year-old Noah was more wisely hesitant, he asked me to help him. I stood in the river, cold water up to my chest, and caught him as he was carried down. I realized my footing was not entirely secure just about the time he realized the water was very fast and over his head. I managed to stabilize myself and we both looked downstream, watching the water continue uncaringly along. We looked at each other and I asked him what he would do if I hadn't been able to catch him. His eyes grew wide and he asked me to help him to the bank where he played happily in the shallower water for the rest of the day. My daughter also played in the shallow water, though much less happily - once again, doing my job as a mom made me mean and uncaring. Oh well. A couple weeks later I took a friend to this same river while my kids were on a short trip with their dad. He and I sat in the middle, in lawn chairs, letting the water pick up our feet as we relaxed for the afternoon. It was so peaceful and the water was so refreshing, I could see why my daughter was annoyed at me for interrupting her swimming.

When I was younger my family and I went camping along the Minam River which is about an hour northeast of La Grande, Oregon. This was great! At that point I was able to rely on the adults to prepare the food, build the fire, choose the campground, and drive us to the starting point so we could float down the Minam with inner-tubes. Oh yes, and set limits and keep us safe, thank-you responsible adults for keeping me alive. My younger brothers Daniel and Hayden and I rode down that river time after time for probably three days. It was so peaceful to bob along as part of the cold water, I would love to go do that again. Of course, as with any camping trip, there was a lot more to keep us happy - a campfire complete with marshmallows and scary stories. Sleeping in tents, eating my dad's delicious camping food (which, for him, is like regular food only cooked on a camp stove), hiking. Listening to owls hoot in the night, being awakened by mourning doves and other birds, seeing deer and mountain goats.

I didn't always have the best of luck with camping. My parents love to tell the story of taking me backpacking when I was three. Apparently I didn't really love the idea of carrying a backpack - even though it only held marshmallows; nor did I like the idea of having to walk and walk and walk. My dad says I would trail behind them, staying consistently about 10 feet behind, but when they would stop to wait for me ..... I would stop too. I do not remember subjecting my parents to this frustration, but to this day my mom hates camping. Could this be why? There is another story everyone loves to tell, the story of the time we went camping and I forgot my shoes. I was about seven years old and I remember never wearing shoes, I still don't, who needs them in the summer, right? But this day no one noticed my unshod feet, so when I jumped out of the van at the camp site there were some pretty annoyed adults. I never really figured out why they minded, what did it matter if my filthy feet brought a little dirt into the tent? Or if I stepped on a thorn? Or a bee? Or another nail? I think I remember my dad having to drive to the nearest town for a pair of shoes for me.

When my children were two and four I bought backpacks so we could carry them on hikes. My dad and brothers Christian and Daniel and I took turns carrying them as we hiked around the Wallowas, they were very heavy but being able to take them on beautiful hikes was worth it. To this day both kids love camping, last year as we were camping at the Oregon Coast my son woke up one morning and told me he wanted to just live like this, camping in a tent, forever. For as much as he dislikes bathing, I can imagine he would probably love it!

Let's go to the Movies

Out on the town. Who doesn't anticipate a romantic, elegant, entertaining, or just plain fun evening out? I so enjoy walking through our lovely downtown, visiting the latest restaurants or stores, seeing friends and visitors. But how our town has changed! When I was a child in the 80's we went to the Eastgate Mall to see and be seen – oh, Hatfields! Fabricland! Payless! And to see a movie we had the Liberty Theatre and the Plaza Twin Cinema. Really, at the time none of these places were really very elegant or even attractive, merely just a reflection of the bustling functionality of the time.

But a generation before it was a different experience altogether. At that time there were no videos, Netflix or on-line movies, there were occasional 8mm home movies, and the Milton Freewater Drive-In theater we are fortunate to still be able to enjoy today, and the Liberty Theater downtown. My Aunt Florene described to me how wonderful it was at that time to go to the Liberty Theater with her husband Barry, "Oh, Barry and I LOVED, LOVED LOVED going to the movies downtown and always sitting in the loges, these really comfy seats in the balcony. It was so cool because you could look down on all the kids below. The bathrooms were old world elegance. It seems like they used to have a maid in there also. Maybe I'm just imagining that. When you walked up and down the stairs, I always felt very glamorous. Especially coming down, alone. We still wore dresses and you could imagine yourself being a movie star coming down the long stairway".

Today you can still see some of the vestiges of the Liberty Theatre. When it was purchased by The Bon Marche (Now Macys) they did a nice job of paying homage to the glory days of cinema. I remember when they first expanded into the movie theatre space in the mid-eighties all the dressing rooms were named after classic movie-stars.

Going to the movies now is no longer as stylish an experience, although it is certainly high-tech and comfortable at The Grand Cinemas, especially if you splurge on a 3D movie.

Going to live theater, however, is still an elegant way to spend an evening just as it was a generation ago. I was lucky enough to attend the Alice Burlesque show at the Powerhouse theater last year. Amazing! Not just the fantastic show, which I can't describe adequately other than to say the women were gorgeous and classy. But the entire experience made me feel, like my Aunt Florene all those years ago, like a celebrity. I wore a cape and a mauve cloche over a fancy red dress. We had wine and visited before the show and partied afterwards with the cast of Alice, while DJ Adam Whiteside played a fun mix of dance music.

The Little Theatre is another part of Walla Walla which has survived from that era, and is still around to be enjoyed today. The Little Theatre seems a little more reserved but equally social and elegant. I recently saw White Christmas featuring a talented and energetic cast. My whole family absolutely loved it.

Walla Walla has changed through the years, but in many ways has stayed the same. Going out on the town is still a wonderful way to experience our lovely city.

The Liberty Theatre is still in downtown, Walla Walla. Sasquatch is not.

The Drive-in

Going to the Drive-in is a special treat that all of us here in the Walla Walla Valley are still lucky enough to enjoy, thanks to the Milton-Freewater Drive-In. Walla Walla used to have a drive-in, too. My aunt, Debbie Mobley, told me the drive-in is one of her favorite childhood memories, "I enjoyed going to the Sky-Vue Drive-In on Friday nights in the old blue station wagon with the whole family. We would take pop corn from home and get a jug of A&W root beer and we always wore our PJ's and played on the swings before the movie started. Dad would sometimes get drive in pizza too. That was always a treat though." My grandparents must have liked the drive-in because I remember going there with them on Friday nights too. I don't remember much more than playing on the swings and the cute cartoons advertising drive-in treats beforehand because I was pretty young when the Sky-Vue closed for good. Now the field where it stood is a trailer court.

I continue the tradition now by taking my two kids to an occasional drive-in movie. The kids still wear their pajamas and play on the playground before the movie, but now we listen to the broadcast over the radio rather than on the little silver speaker that hooked on the window. Plus we always buy treats at the concession stand, I love movie popcorn and my kids love Red Ropes. We usually leave before the second show, though if it is a grown up movie it's nice to be able to let the kids fall asleep but still be able to watch on my own. And since they're already in their jammies, all I have to do is carry them to their beds when we get home.

Cow/Elk Love

Even Elks need love

Love is in the air. With Valentine's Day fast approaching, talk of love is circling in all aspects of my life. I like to look for connections in things, and this morning when I opened an email from Joe Drazan, our local historian, I laughed when I saw a picture of what looked like a love tryst between the Elk and the Cow. Imagine the effort that went into that 1983 prank. I mentioned the spectacle of the elk/cow mix-up in a previous essay and in my memory I got it confused, I imagined the Elk had gone to visit the Cow at 4-J's....turns out she was the instigator in that relationship! The romantic part of me loves the idea of these two cooking up a midnight rendezvous, with the cow sneaking over to see her dear elk on his elegant building.

The Elks was one of Nanny and Fafa's, regular Friday night places. The two of them always knew how to have a good time; they went out every Friday night from the time they got married. Nanny still goes out with friends on Friday night, though Fafa has now passed away. I asked her about her memories of The Elks and she said, "For one thing it wasn't there...it was downtown, on Alder. When Fafa and I used to go to the Elks we would go up a bunch of stairs and it was on a top floor. We had fun. We would dance and eat. They had a band, seems like I remember doing the Twist there." My mom also remembers going to the original Elks, she attended ballroom dance classes with her friends Candy and Cindy Beck and he recalls the elegance of the building. When I looked on Joe Drazan's Bygone Walla Walla website I was surprised (and a little sad) to see that the original building, located on 4th and Alder, was torn down in the Summer of 1973. The photographs show a beautiful building with curved ceilings, chandeliers, and a fireplace –different from the building we have today!

My cousin, Karie, had her wedding reception at the Elk's about fifteen years ago. It was a great place for our enormous family, especially because the dance floor is so large and we are a family of dancers! My 10th class reunion was also held at the Elks, we had so much fun and enjoyed excellent food – plus made use of that dance floor again.

And the Elks is still going on strong today. I had a lot of friends attend a concert there on New Year's Eve. One even had a midnight kiss with a stranger in a cowboy hat. What kind of love current is in the air at the Elks? Today, the noble Elk still stands guard on his building....but I don't know where the Cow is. I hope he isn't too heartbroken, he looks like he may be searching for her still.

Together, though only for a moment

Weddings

Playing dignified bachelorette games

    I've been lucky enough to attend some beautiful weddings lately. I enjoy weddings so much that I often find myself pretty involved. I love the bridal shower when we give the bride-to-be slinky gifts. I love the bachelorette party where we get to wear badges saying Flirt! or Lucky! while playing honeymoon-themed games. I love picking out crystal bowls and towels as wedding gifts. I love dressing up for the reception and seeing everyone at the wedding.

But this all pales in comparison to the actual wedding. The sheer variety for each couple couple creates happy anticipation. Will it be a formal wedding with a fancy reception? Will it be low-key? Will it be fun? One never knows. It is never the amount spent, either, it is the people and the energy surrounding the event. The creative ideas: one bride had delightful tutus at the church entrance so each little girl could be a flower girl. Isn't that a great idea? This same young lady and her husband also had a candy table at the reception. Another couple pulled out all the stops - formal ceremony, lovely country club reception, every detail beautiful - though their genuine love and high regard the family shared for one another is what made the event particularly wonderful.

Informal weddings are equally fun and beautiful. One young and very much in love couple had an outdoor ceremony under a hand-made altar followed by the groom and several of the groomsmen jumping into the swimming pool before sending the couple off under fireworks. (I suspect the men were looking for a way to get out of their formal clothing.)

My favorites, though, are the out of character weddings. The hippie couple taking solemn vows in a Catholic church under dad's loving but disciplined gaze. The free spirit whose much more conservative older siblings made her change when she put on a strapless sundress at the reception. The rebellious punk looking like Grace Kelly in her mother's wedding dress. Seeing my friends and family all dressed up in suits and dresses sharing a meaningful event with grandmothers and little kids make weddings such a treat.

A toast to you, brides and grooms, may your love continue to grow!

Nanny's 85th Birthday

My family loves having fun, we look for any excuse for a party and run with it. Recently my grandma turned 85 and we had quite the shindig. Nanny didn't want a party, and she ended up getting her own way when she had a dizzy spell within the first ten minutes of the party and had to go to the hospital. What had been planned as a huge event with everybody coming from miles around, tables full of food, a "bomb" fire, and Jello Shots started out as just a very nervous gathering as we waited to hear from my aunt and uncle if she was OK. It didn't take too long for them to get back to us that, yes, she was just fine, she just had low sodium levels and needed to spend the night in the hospital and wanted us to all just go ahead and have fun. Never people to pass up a good time (or tremendous quantities of Jello Shots) we obeyed.

In typical Mobley fashion there was way more food than anyone could eat and way more to drink than anyone could drink. We sat around the bon fire and talked and joked and told stories while all the little kids ran around and played zombie tag. I find it interesting that when I was a child we played Cops and Robbers and my parents played Cowboys and Indians but my poor children are playing Zombie tag. Thanks a lot World War Z. Were robbers or indians ever even remotely as terrifying as zombies? I guess maybe before people had the idea of zombies chewing their brains up. And how do my kids know about this, anyway? No way do I let them watch horror movies, but somehow when I was reading World War Z (which is absolutely terrifying) my kids got the idea that this zombie invasion idea was a real situation. This is entirely my fault and now I have to deal with it. Here's what happened: I would talk to people about this book, saying things like, "Isn't it amazing how Israel dealt with the issue so quickly? I was really impressed when I read about Israel, zombies wouldn't stand a chance there." To which my mom or friend or whoever would calmly respond, "Yes, but I felt so bad for the mother who was just watching TV with her family when they came busting through the windows."

My kids, wide-eyed, would overhear these literary conversations and believe that zombies were indeed invading our world. Shoot, I'm so sorry children. They may be scarred for life. Luckily I took them to see a little kid movie called 'ParaNorman' not too long after I inadvertently contributed to their lifelong nightmares. Thankfully ParaNorman has some zombie characters in it that are sweet and harmless, just misunderstood. Maybe the creators of that cartoon were tired of having to comfort their kids in the middle of the night too, who knows, I just know that now my kids have a normal fear of zombies instead of an obsession.

But I've gotten off topic. At my Nanny's 85th birthday party we had Jello Shooters, but they wouldn't end. They were like the brooms in the Sorcerers Apprentice, marching out endlessly, simply multiplying into more Jello Shots the more we drank. Luckily this was an all day event with lots of food so no one was too affected, but by the end of the evening the conversation turned to politics which is never a good combination with liquor. Or parties. Or families. Or anything that is supposed to be fun.

Being a peacemaker, I got up and walked away as soon as someone (let's just say it might have been Tom Alexenko) brought up his political views. I went and made sure my kids had gone home safely with my parents for the evening, helped with some clean up, and then returned to the bomb fire. They were still talking about politics. In fact there was an obvious divide with one half of the fire standing for one side and one half of the family standing for another. My cousin Chad and I both kept trying to change the subject, and not because we don't have political views, in fact he and I routinely cancel each other out in the ballot box; but because we both enjoy parties, socializing, and having fun. And arguing about politics is definitely not fun. But our attempts were ignored and the conversation got more and more passionate. Thankfully we all really care about each other and everyone is respectful so nothing came of it other than an eventual bet (complete with a photograph and a handshake) over who would be the next president. I was relieved when the discussion ended, in fact there was a moment there when the heated political discussion was starting to scare me more than the idea of a zombie invasion.

The sparks fly as Tom and Paul make their official bet while Marcy checks validity

Jello Shooters

Jello Shooters

Ingredients

3-Ounce Box Jello
1 Cup Boiling Water
1/2 Cup Liquor (see below)
1/2 Cup Cold Water

Flavor Combinations
- Lemon Jello and Citrus Vodka
- Lime Jello and Gin
- Mixed Fruit Jello and Vodka
- Strawberry Jello and Rum

Directions

Stir boiling water into Jello until dissolved and cooled, add water then liquor. Add to plastic shot-sized cups and refrigerate at least 2 hours. Avoid serving to people who might disagree about politics.

Birthday Parties

Who doesn't love a kid birthday party? The cake, the presents, the gift bags, the kids who refuse to go home at the end of the party. Now that I have been a mom for over nine years I have been to many, many kid parties. I have also thrown many kids parties. I could probably write an entire book on kid parties. When and how to create the invitations, what to put in the gift bags, what to serve, where to have the party, who to invite, how to decorate, when to serve the cake, what games to serve. It is a definite art.

For a long time all the parents went too, this was fun! We would stand around and watch our kids play, we helped them pass out their presents and say thank you, we wiped spilled juice and surreptitiously ate half-eaten pieces of cake. We were part of the action too and I, for one, really enjoyed it. But then my daughter turned eight and one day as we were walking into the Jumpy Castle venue for the latest birthday party she turned to me and said, "Mom, you can just drop me off. The other mom's aren't even going to be here."

What!?? I'm not invited? Noah and I were just kind of dumbstruck, what were we supposed to do? For this particular party I insisted that no one would care if we stayed (they didn't) and since I was paying for Noah separately it would be like we just happened to be there too. So we got to crash that last birthday party. Darn it. It hadn't occurred to me all those years ago that the day would come when suddenly I have to fill two hours of my time. Thankfully Noah, at six, still lets me crash his parties, but I think I will probably bow out a little sooner this time so he doesn't have to dump me like Natalie did. I may have to start actually asking him if I can attend with him, kind of a pre-emptive preparation for the time when he won't want me to be a big part of his social life either.

Man I'm going to need a hobby.

Being a Kid

My mom, standing, her sister, Debbie, and Grandma Mac.
Grandparents have always existed to spoil grandkids.

What is it that makes kids, well, kids? I spend about 95% of my time around kids, and this somehow does not make me a kid myself. In fact, I am most decidedly NOT a kid. At work I am the one telling people to stay on task, pay attention, turn things in, sit correctly, mmmnnnnmmnnaaammmna (that was the Charlie Brown teacher voice).

Then I go home and I do the same thing. Wake up, make your bed, clean that up, let's go, mmmmnnannannaha (there's that Charlie Brown teacher voice again). It is clear to me that I am often the only person in the room not having fun. Hrrmmph.

Going to the beach is fun, no matter your age. I have to admit, though, as a child it may have been more carefree - in fact, I can't think of anything more carefree than jumping into the Pacific Ocean when it is fifty degrees and raining. As a kid, you know your mom will be there with a towel and warm clothes when you emerge from the freezing cold water nearly blue, teeth chattering. That same mom will also carry your shoes and wet jeans as well as get you all snuggly by the campfire with hot chocolate after a hot shower and jammies. So why would any kid not jump in the ocean? But as an adult if I were to jump in the ocean I would probably still be wet and shivering a couple of days later as I searched around for dry clothes. That's ok, I will console myself with beautiful vistas from hikes, eating fresh-caught crab, and the joy of watching my kids play in the sand.

It's not just the beach that's easier for kids, a lot of things are like that. Restaurants, for example. As a kid, going to a restaurant was easy: eat a little bite of food then go run around, maybe play with the cigarette dispenser or make a couple of collect phone calls from the pay phone while the adults chatted. Fun. Now? Ugh. Trying to keep little kids seated long enough to actually eat an entire meal, keeping them occupied while waiting for the meal, and the worst, keeping them seated and quiet while adults slowly finish their meal. Crayons and color sheets are enjoyable, for oh, four minutes. Jelly packets offer another two or three minutes of amusement. Then a trip to the bathroom can kill another ten if the kids can be entertained by hand washing and air dryers and possibly a fish tank or some artwork on the walls. If we're lucky the food will have arrived by this point, unless - horrors! - some well-meaning but inexperienced waiter brings the kids' food early. But in an ideal restaurant situation everyone gets their food at the same time and the kids are occupied for another two or three minutes before one needs to go to the bathroom again or the other wants to walk around and visit with other diners. Taking very young children to restaurants isn't all that much fun, though sometimes it is unavoidable when it is a family dinner or we are traveling. Now that they are school-age my kids are great in restaurants, they are able to sit and visit without any distraction besides a visit or two to the rest room.

The fair, too, may be the best example of AWESOME for kids while simultaneously being AWFUL for parents. Not to knock the fair, I love it. I love the gut-bomb food, the animals, the crafts and plants and vegetables. I love the 4-H exhibits, talking to people I haven't seen since last year, the demolition derby, the concert, the rodeo, the beer garden, the horses, the local performances. Notice no where did I say I love spending hundreds of dollars on bracelets so my kids can ride bumpy, nauseating rides. I may have also omitted cotton candy. And face painting. Oh, did I forget the booths where you can buy stuff? Wait, no, I didn't actually forget those things because I am not nine years old. For a child, going to the fair is about the rides, the junk food, the face paint, and the cool treasures you can buy. That is it. Animals? Handicrafts? Machines? What? What? I remember this as a kid. My grandparents are (darn it, were) fun-loving people who loved to go to the horse races. Plus they loved us. The fair let them combine these two loves with one fell swoop: toss a whole bunch of money at us, then head to the races! Everyone was happy. We ran wild, and if we needed money we just went looking for Nanny and Fafa, they never said no. Sigh. Why can't I be like that? I'm a mean mommy! Oh, wait, maybe I just can't afford it. It is all the same to a kid. Just another way kids get to skate through life.

And kids do get to skate through life. Literally. Have you ever seen an adult on a skateboard? Me neither. There was that rumor that Tony Hawk was 40 doing those tricks, but I think that's bald-faced lies told by kids who hope they can skate when they're 40. Or gymnastics? Sure, I can do a cartwheel, but I'm always extremely proud of myself afterward. I don't do a cartwheel simply to do a cartwheel anymore. Now it's more like a challenge or a reminder, a "wait, can I still do a cartwheel?" thing. Though now that I think of it, I guess the biggest difference between kids and adults, besides their obvious really nice skin and amazing exuberance for everything and also their complete disregard for grown up stuff like being clean or on time or planning ahead or paying for things, is that kids are energetic and healthy. Physical fitness. Yes. If I wake up tomorrow at 5:30 in the morning and put my tennis shoes on I will be energetic and healthy too. Yes! This will happen! Soon I will be running around restaurants talking to strangers, not paying my bill, gazing at fish tanks, jumping into freezing oceans while someone else carries my clothes before riding the squirrel cage ride. Yes!! Being a kid is all about energy and health. I run tomorrow.

How about these guys being kids?
Boys in the 1950's really knew how to get out there and enjoy life.

And now...

As I near middle age (gah! Did I just write that?) I am so much more content. I don't feel old, I feel as eager for life as I did when I was a young teen. I still love to sing and dance and eat meals with people. I still enjoy a good party and cute clothes. I still enjoy sharing a joke with my friends. Only now I realize I have my whole family to enjoy life with, including two little kids. I am happy and so thankful to live in Walla Walla.

Under the sparkling tourist-town veneer, Walla Walla is still my same hometown where I can enjoy the beauty of the valley, the trees, and the lovely architecture. I can participate in the cultural events and fun activities. When I was in junior high my dad wore that bright yellow shirt that he won at a radio contest that said I ❤ ❤ Walla Walla and I would cringe....but now I would wear it with pride.

I love love Walla Walla. And I bet Walla Walla even loves me back.

Thank you to my family for your support, especially my mom for encouraging me to have the confidence to continue with writing and my dad for revising with such care. Thank you to Florene for reading and your feedback. Thank you to Joe Drazan for allowing me to include some photographs from your Bygone Walla Walla project, I really enjoy your blog. Thank you to Tom Skeen and Brenden Koch for including my articles in the Union Bulletin. Thank you to Mrs. Westerguard and Mrs. Bledsoe, two teachers who allowed me to write and write and write….

A great big thank you to my family and friends who are my source of inspiration. I will make you dinner if I mixed up your story (ha ha, then I can get a new one!)

Thank you to Paul for believing in me. And a great big thank you to Natalie and Noah for simply being you.

About the Author

Sara Van Donge is a writer, teacher, and mom whose passion for her hometown is evident in her debut book. She writes for her local newspaper as well as two blogs, Deja Views and Tastes and Tours. Sara lives with her family next to a small stream in Walla Walla. She enjoys shared meals, attending sporting events, and watching dogs be silly.

33518105R00144

Made in the USA
San Bernardino, CA
04 May 2016